### SID MEIER'S
# CIVILIZATION III ®

# SID MEIER'S CIVILIZATION III

FIRAXIS
GAMES

INFOGRAMES

Infogrames, Inc.
417 Fifth Avenue
New York, NY 10016 USA

MADE IN THE USA.

First Edition, September 2001

10 9 8 7 6 5 4 3 2 1

# CONTENTS

CHAPTER 1

## GAME REQUIREMENTS AND INSTALLATION 1

# CHAPTER 2

## INTRODUCTION 5

# CHAPTER 3

## SETTING UP A GAME 11

# CHAPTER 4

## FOR BEGINNERS ONLY           **21**

# CHAPTER 5

## IF YOU'VE PLAYED BEFORE     **37**

# CHAPTER 6

## THE BASICS OF TOWNS AND CITIES     **47**

# CHAPTER 7

# TERRAIN AND MOVEMENT             59

## CHAPTER

**UNITS**      **75**

# CHAPTER 9

## CIVILIZATION ADVANCES $\qquad$ 91

# CHAPTER 10

## WONDERS $\qquad$ 99

# CHATER

## Managing Your Cities                                    **103**

# CHAPTER 12

## MANAGING YOUR EMPIRE                                    121

# CHAPTER 13

## DIPLOMACY AND TRADE                                     135

# CHAPTER 14

## WINNING THE GAME          151

# CHAPTER

---

## REFERENCE: SCREEN BY SCREEN      **155**

# APPENDICES

# GAME REQUIREMENTS AND INSTALLATION

*"Even the tallest tower begins with the first stone."*

In the beginning…the Earth was without form and void. It will stay that way until you install the game and start playing. Here's how.

## Requirements

Before you install the *Civilization® III* CD-ROM game, make sure your computer has everything you need:

- 300 MHz Pentium® II processor or better (for best performance, we recommend at least a 500 MHz Pentium II);

- At least 32 MB (megabytes) of RAM (for best performance, we recommend 64 MB or more);

- 4X speed CD-ROM drive (or faster);

- Video card compatible with DirectX® 8.0a and capable of at least 1024 x 768 resolution and 16-bit color depth;

- Sound card compatible with DirectX 8.0a;

- Mouse (or some other device that fulfills the same function);

- Windows® 95, Windows 98, Windows Me, Windows 2000, or Windows XP;

- DirectX 8.0a (which you can install as part of the installation process); and

- Sufficient empty space on your hard drive. How much you need depends on how much of the game you choose to install. The minimum required is 500 MB (plus an additional 50 MB for the swap file).

If you think you have all of this, but still have a problem running the game, please contact Technical Support for assistance.

## Installing

If you have all of the required equipment and software, then it's time to install the game. To do so, follow these instructions:

- Turn on your computer, open the CD-ROM drive, place the *Civilization III* CD-ROM in it, and close the drive.

- This is a Windows "AutoPlay" CD-ROM. That means that just putting the disc in the drive for the first time starts up the AutoPlay program. In the window that opens, select "Install Civilization III" to begin.

### If AutoPlay Doesn't Work

If, for whatever reason, the AutoPlay feature doesn't work when you put the CD-ROM in the drive, here's how to start the installation program yourself:

- Double-click your "My Computer" desktop icon.

- In the window that opens, double-click your CD-ROM drive.

- In the list that appears, find a file named **setup.exe** and double-click it.

The installation program should begin.

- Click Install to continue. (If you change your mind at this point, click Exit instead.)

- Read the End User License Agreement and, if you accept the terms, click Next to continue the installation.

- Choose the folder where you want to install the game. You can accept the default or use the Browse button to select a different folder. Click Next when you're done.

- To add the game to your Windows Start menu, choose a Program Folder to put it in. The default is *Civilization III*. Click Next to continue.

- Decide what sort of installation you want to do. You have the option of doing a Standard installation or a Minimum one. If your hard drive space is limited, use Minimum. This option leaves nonessential files on the CD-ROM (which results in a reduction in performance).

- Once you've made your choices, the installation program copies the files to your hard drive from the CD-ROM, then creates the new program group and icons.

- Last, you can electronically register your new game by following the onscreen instructions.

# Playing

Once the automated installation and setup are complete, you're ready to start making history. To begin:

- Make sure the CD-ROM is in your drive.

- Double-click the *Civilization III* icon on your desktop or select the game from the Start menu.

# INTRODUCTION

*"There are so many worlds, and I have not yet conquered even one."*

## Five Impulses of Civilization

There is no single driving force behind the urge toward civilization, no one goal toward which every culture strives. There is, instead, a web of forces and objectives that impel and beckon, shaping cultures as they grow. In the *Civilization III* game, five basic impulses are of the greatest importance to the health and flexibility of your fledgling society.

## Exploration

An early focus in the game is exploration. You begin the game knowing almost nothing about your surroundings. Most of the map is dark. Your units move into this darkness of unexplored territory and discover new terrain; mountains, rivers, grasslands, and forests are just some of the features they might find. The areas they explore might be occupied by minor tribes or another culture's units. In either case, a chance meeting might provoke a variety of encounters.

## Economics

As your civilization expands, you'll need to manage the growing complexity of its production and resource requirements. Adjusting the tax rates and choosing the most productive terrain for your purposes, you can control the speeds at which your population grows larger and your cities produce goods. By setting taxes higher and science lower, you can tilt your economy into a cash cow. You can also adjust the happiness of your population. Perhaps you'll assign more of your population to entertainment, or you might clamp down on unrest with a larger military presence. You can establish trade with other powers to bring in luxuries and strategic resources to satisfy the demands of your empire.

## Knowledge

On the flip side of your economics management is your commitment to scholarship. By setting taxes lower and science higher, you can increase the frequency with which your population discovers new technologies. With each new advance, further paths of learning open up and new units and city improvements become available for manufacture. Some technological discoveries let your cities build unique Wonders of the World.

## Conquest

Perhaps your taste runs to military persuasion. The *Civilization III* game allows you to pursue a range of postures, from pure defense through imperialistic aggression to cooperative alliance. One way to win the game is to be the last civilization standing when the dust clears. Of course, first you must overcome both fierce barbarian attacks and swift sorties by your opponents.

## Culture

When a civilization becomes stable and prosperous enough, it can afford to explore the Arts. Though cultural achievements often have little practical value, they are frequently the measure by which history—and other cultures—judge a people. A strong culture also helps to build a cohesive society that can resist assimilation by an occupying force. The effort you spend on building an enduring cultural identity might seem like a luxury, but without it, you forfeit any chance at a greatness other civilizations will respect.

# The Big Picture

A winning strategy is one that combines all of these aspects into a flexible whole. Your first mission is to survive; your second is to thrive. It is not true that the largest civilization is necessarily the winner, nor that the wealthiest always has the upper hand. In fact, a balance of knowledge, cash, military might, cultural achievement, and diplomatic ties allows you to respond to any crisis that occurs, whether it is a barbarian invasion, an aggressive rival, or an upsurge of internal unrest.

# Winning

There are now more ways of winning the game. You can still win the Space Race with fast research and a factory base devoted to producing spacecraft components. You can still conquer the world by focusing on a strong military strategy. If you dominate the great majority of the globe, your rival may well give in to your awesome might.

In addition, there's a purely Diplomatic means of success; if you're universally renowned as a trustworthy peacemaker, you can become head of the United Nations. Then there's the challenge of overwhelming the world with your Cultural achievements—not an easy task.

Finally, of course, is perhaps the most satisfying victory of all—beating your own highest Histographic Civilization Score or those of your friends. See **Chapter 14: Winning the Game** for an in-depth analysis of the scoring system.

# The Documentation

The folks who make computer games know that most players never read the manual. Until a problem rears its head, the average person just bulls through by trial and error; it's part of the fun. When a problem does come up, this type of player wants to spend as little time in the book as possible, then get back to the game. For those of you who are looking for a quick fix, **Chapter 15: Reference: Screen by Screen** is the place to go.

For the rest of you, we've tried to organize the chapters in the order that you'll need them if you've never played a *Civilization* game before. If you're new to the game, the sidebars on concepts should help you understand the fundamentals of the game.

The **Readme** file on the CD-ROM has the rundown on the very latest changes, things that didn't make it into this manual. (Due to printing and binding time, the manual has to be completed before final tweaks are made.)

Last but not least, the *Civilization III* game continues the tradition of including a vast compendium of onscreen help. Click on the Civilopedia icon (the book near your advisors) or on any hyperlinked text in the game to open the Civilopedia. This handy reference includes entries describing all the units, improvements, governments, terrain, general game concepts, and more—everything you could want to know about the *Civilization* world. The entries are hyperlinked so you can jump from one to another with ease.

## Interface Conventions

You play the *Civilization III* game using a combination of both mouse and keyboard. Many people find that the shortcut keys significantly speed up their play.

### Using a Mouse

Throughout the text, we assume that you understand basic mouse functions and terms, like "click and drag." Since not everybody knows these things, here are brief definitions of how we use the most common terms:

- "Click" means to place the mouse pointer over an area of the screen and click the left mouse button.

- "Right-click" is to click with the right mouse button.

- "Click and hold" means to hold down the mouse button.

- "Drag" is to hold a button down while moving the mouse.

- "Select" means to click on something.

- "Press (a button)" means to click on one of the onscreen buttons.

- "Scroll" is (1) to drag the button along a slider bar to see more information than an onscreen box can hold, or (2) to place the mouse pointer at the edge of the screen so that the map "scrolls" to show a different area.

**The Map:** The game uses an isometric grid. This means each terrain square (also called a *tile*) is roughly diamond shaped, as if you are viewing it from an angle. Movement proceeds along the eight points of the compass (up, down, left, right, and the diagonals). Some players have difficulty getting used to this view, finding it hard, for example, to tell where a city's radius begins and ends. If you have this problem, try using the Show Map Grid option ([Ctrl]-[G]). This outlines each map square with a thin border.

**Shortcut keys:** Almost all of the orders and options have a shortcut ([R] for Roads, for example). Pressing this key or combination of keys has the same effect as clicking the order or option. We mention the keys throughout the manual, and they're listed in **Chapter 15: Reference: Screen by Screen** too.

**Cursors:** The mouse pointer, or cursor, has a few different shapes in the game, depending on your current game task.

Your normal cursor is usually visible. You use this just like you normally do—to click on options, buttons, and so on

A flashing highlight around a unit indicates that this is the active unit. Use the number keypad on your keyboard to order this unit to move—or you can click an order to give the unit other orders.

When you give a unit the order to Bombard, your cursor changes to cross-hairs. Use the cross-hairs to select the target of the bombardment. (If the cursor becomes anything other than cross-hairs, you've moved it outside the effective range of the bombardment.) Only certain units have this ability; check the Civilopedia entry for a unit if you suspect it might be capable of bombardment.

A number and a trail leading back to the active unit indicates that when you release the mouse button, the active unit will begin moving toward the indicated square. See "GoTo Orders" in **Chapter 7: Terrain and Movement** for complete details.

When you give a unit the order to Paradrop, your cursor changes to a parachute. Use this to select the target square for the drop; a crossed-out chute indicates that the square your cursor is over is not a valid target. See "Airdrop Orders" in **Chapter 7: Terrain and Movement** for complete details.

Some text in the game contains hyperlinks to the Civilopedia. Click with the hand icon to jump to that entry.

**Dialog box buttons:** When a dialog box is onscreen, click the circle icon for OK or the X icon for Cancel.

# SETTING UP A GAME

*"If I had the power to remake the world…ahh, but that is folly."*

When you launch the game, the opening animation begins. You can watch it through, or you can click the left mouse button or press any key to cut it short.

Beginning a game means choosing the circumstances in which you want to play. Your options include specifying the number of opponents and customizing the world you'll explore.

## Your First Decision

Setting up a game means making easy decisions on a series of options screens. The first menu is where it all begins.

**New Game:** Begin an entirely new game. Choosing this option means going through the pre-game options screens, which we explain below.

**Quick Start:** Start a new game using the same game settings as the last New Game played.

**Tutorial:** Start a new game, with a random civilization, on the easiest difficulty setting. During the game, you'll get helpful advice designed to ease new players into the game.

**Load Game:** Load and continue a previously saved game. A dialog box lists all of the saved games available. Choose the game you wish to load.

**Load Scenario:** Load a scenario. You can create your own game scenarios or play scenarios your friends have constructed to challenge you. To load successfully, scenarios *must* have been created with the *Civilization III* CD-ROM game. Older scenarios from other *Civilization* games are not compatible.

**Hall of Fame:** See the standings attained by the most successful rulers in previous games.

**Preferences:** Set game preferences.

**Audio Preferences:** Set volume levels for audio options.

**Credits:** Find out who's responsible for creating the game.

**Exit:** Quit the game.

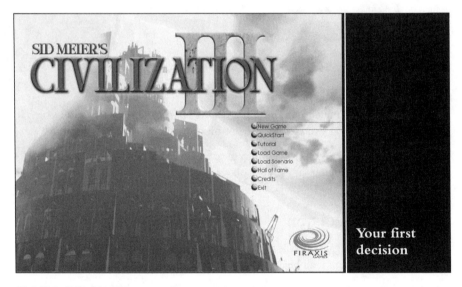

Double-click the option you choose.

## Choose Your World

If you choose New Game, the next two screens allow you to set up the game the way you want it to be. The first of these gives you control over all the important aspects of the planet that you'll be exploring. There are a number of options, which we'll describe in a moment.

When you are happy with all your choices, click the O button to continue to that screen. To return to the Main menu, click the X button.

**Land Mass and Water Coverage**

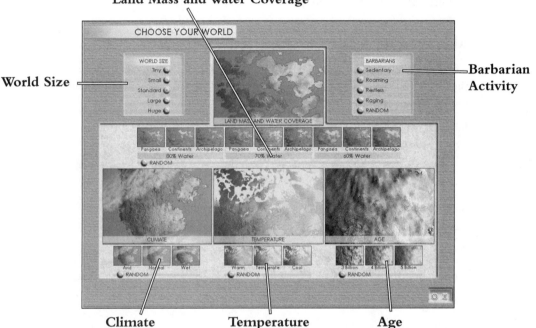

World Size

Barbarian Activity

Climate    Temperature    Age

## World Size

By choosing the size of the map, you determine how much territory there is and, to a large degree, how long the game takes to play.

**Tiny:** This size map leads to short, intensely contested games. Tribes find each other quickly.

**Small:** These games are slightly less intense than those on tiny maps. You'll still run into your opponents quickly.

**Standard:** This is the standard size map.

**Large:** This sprawling map takes longer to explore and exploit. Consequently, games go on longer.

**Huge:** Games played on this size map allow plenty of development time before tribes meet one another. Wars tend to be prolonged and tough. You'll have to work hard to dominate this size world before you run out of game time.

## Land Mass and Water Coverage

This option sets the percentage of terrain squares that are water versus land, as well as the form of that land. There are three Water Coverage settings, each with three potential Land Mass settings.

**80% Ocean:** Choosing this option gives your world a small number of land squares and a larger number of ocean squares.

**70% Ocean:** This option yields land and ocean squares roughly equivalent to that of our own Earth.

**60% Ocean:** This option produces a larger number of land squares and a small number of ocean squares.

**Archipelago:** This option produces large numbers of relatively small continents.

**Continents:** This option yields a few large land masses and a few smaller ones.

**Pangaea:** Choosing this gives you one large supercontinent.

**Random:** This option randomly selects settings for Water Coverage and Land Mass.

## Climate

This parameter sets the relative frequency with which particular terrain types—especially Desert and Jungle—occur.

**Arid:** Choosing this option gives your world a larger number of dry terrain squares, such as Plains and Desert.

**Normal:** This option yields about equal numbers of wet and dry terrain squares.

**Wet:** This option produces a larger number of wet terrain squares, such as Jungle and Flood Plain.

**Random:** Use this option if you want the Climate setting chosen for you.

## Age

This parameter determines how long erosion, continental drift, and tectonic activity have had to sculpt your world.

**3 Billion Years:** This option yields a young, rough world, in which terrain types occur in clusters.

**4 Billion Years:** This option yields a middle-aged world, one in which plate tectonics have been acting to diversify terrain.

**5 Billion Years:** This option produces an old world, one in which the tectonics have settled down somewhat, allowing erosion and other natural forces to soften the terrain features.

**Random:** This option selects an Age setting at random.

## Temperature

This parameter determines the relative frequency with which particular terrain types occur.

**Cool:** This option produces larger numbers of cold and cool terrain squares, like Tundra.

**Temperate:** Choosing this option gives your world an average number of each terrain type.

**Warm:** This option yields a larger amount of tropical terrain, like Deserts and Jungles.

**Random:** This option selects a Temperature setting at random.

## Barbarian

You can also set the level of barbarian activity in the game.

**Villages:** Players who really hate barbarians can choose to play in this ideal world. Barbarians are restricted to their encampments. The surrounding terrain is free of their mischief.

**Roaming:** Barbarian settlements occasionally appear, but less frequently and in smaller numbers than at higher levels. This is the standard level of barbarian activity.

**Restless:** Barbarians appear in moderate up to significant numbers, at shorter intervals than at lower levels.

**Raging:** You asked for it! The world is full of barbarians, and they appear in large numbers.

**Random:** This option randomly selects a Barbarian setting.

## Player Setup

The second screen of options is where you decide who you'll be and how tough a challenge you're ready for. You can also customize the way the game works. In the center is your Leader Portrait, a preview of how you'll appear to other civilizations in the game. All around it are the various options, which we'll describe in a moment.

When you are happy with all your choices, click the O icon to begin the game. To return to the World Setup screen, select the X icon.

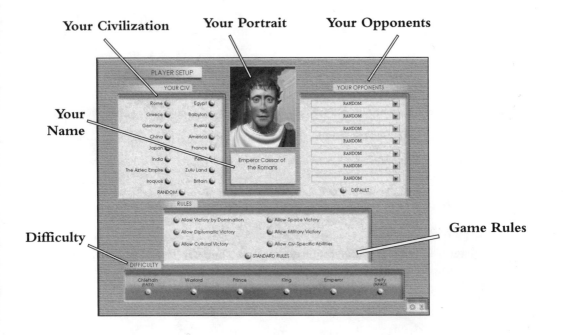

**Prince:** At this difficulty level, everything comes much less easily and your rivals are significantly better at managing their empires. You need some experience and skill to win.

**Monarch:** Experienced and skilled players often play at this level, where the crafty enemy leaders and the unstable attitude of your citizens combine to present a significant challenge.

**Emperor:** This level is for those who feel the need to be humbled. Your opponents will no longer pull their punches; if you want to win, you'll have to earn it.

**Deity:** This is the ultimate *Civilization* challenge, for those who think they've learned to beat the game. You'll have to give a virtuoso performance to survive at this level (and yes, it is possible—theoretically—to win on Deity level). Good luck!

## Game Rules

Tweaking the parameters of the game can change the whole flavor of the challenge. The custom rules offer several different possibilities. (If you mess up, you can reset to the default standards by clicking Standard Rules.)

**Allow Victory by Domination:** If this box is checked, players can win by conquering and controlling two-thirds of the world's territory. The other civilizations, or what's left of them, capitulate to your rule.

**Allow Diplomatic Victory:** Unless this option is unchecked, leaders can win by purely diplomatic means. To be successful, a ruler must be elected Secretary-General through a vote of the United Nations.

**Allow Cultural Victory:** Make sure this option is checked, and any civilization can win the game through overwhelming cultural dominance. For success, a nation must have achieved a certain level of cultural advancement.

**Allow Space Victory:** When this box is checked, players can build spaceship parts and win the game by being the first to launch a spaceship bound for Alpha Centauri.

**Allow Military Victory:** If this box is checked, players can win by eliminating all rival nations. If you're the last one standing, you rule the world.

**Allow Civ-Specific Abilities:** This option controls the diversity factor. When it's checked, each civilization has it own unique strengths and weaknesses (as listed earlier in this section). Turning this off is handy for leveling the playing field.

## Ready, Set, Go

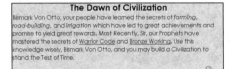

When you are satisfied with your settings, click the O icon to start your game. A box pops up welcoming you to your position as leader and detailing the accomplishments of your culture thus far. When you finish reading the screen, press [Enter] or click the O icon to begin ruling.

## Saving, Quitting, and Loading Games

Like it or not, there comes a time when you have to take a break from the game. You don't want to lose all of your progress, however, so you'll need to save your game. To save your current situation, press [Ctrl]-[S] or click the Menu icon, open the Game menu, and select Save Game. You're given the opportunity to name your saved game. When you're done, you're returned to the game.

To leave the game, press [Esc] or click the Menu icon and select Quit from the Game menu. Remember, unless you save it first, your current game will be lost when you quit. If you want to resign as well as quit, press [Ctrl]-[Q] or select the Resign option instead. This way, your final score is calculated and, if it's high enough, entered into the record books.

If you want to quit your current game but not leave *Civilization III*, start a new game by pressing [Ctrl]-[Shift]-[Q] or selecting New Game from the Game menu. Unless you save it first, your current game will be lost when you quit.

To load a previously saved game, press [Ctrl]-[L] or click the Menu icon and select Load Game from the Game menu. Unless you save it first, your current game will be lost when you load another game.

# FOR BEGINNERS ONLY

*"One clear example is worth more than a warehouse full of inscribed clay tablets."*

First of all, we'd like to welcome you to the ***Civilization*** family. The game is easy to learn, but we've found that it helps to introduce new players to the basic elements. That's what this chapter is for. To make it more interesting, we'll use an imaginary sample game to illustrate the main points. Keep in mind that this is a simple introduction to the game, and it only touches briefly on game concepts. If you want more information on anything, detailed descriptions can be found in the other sections of this manual.

## Building Your First City

To begin, let's assume we've started a game at Chieftain level, the easiest difficulty option available. The game starts on the first turn, in 4000 BC. Your civilization consists of a band of wandering homesteaders, a Settler, and their industrious companions, a Worker. (You could also have a Scout, but not in this imaginary game.) Your first task is to move the Settler to a site that is suitable for the construction of your first city.

Finding suitable locations for cities, especially your first, is one of the most important decisions you make in the game. In order to survive and grow, each city must have access to all three resource types: food (represented by bread), production (represented by shields), and income from commerce (represented by coins). The map is divided into individual "squares," each of which contains a specific type of terrain. Each terrain type yields the three resources in differing amounts. A good city site provides a variety of

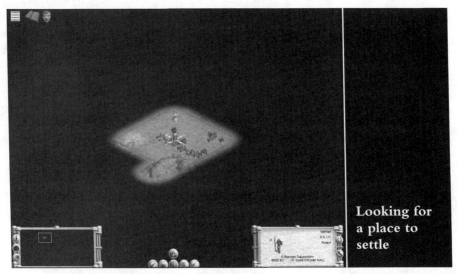

resources. Normally, the lines dividing the map squares are invisible. To see how the terrain is divided, turn on the map grid by pressing [Ctrl]-[G]. Press [Ctrl]-[G] again to remove the grid lines.

Before you move your Settler, take the time to examine the surrounding terrain. Right-click on any unoccupied, visible square, and a pop-up opens. It lists the terrain type, any features in the square, and the output you can expect from the terrain.

Note that only nine map squares are visible. This represents the extent to which your civilization has explored the world. The surrounding dark areas represent unexplored terrain. You can build a city on any terrain square except for water (Coast, Sea, and Ocean) or Mountains. As mentioned earlier, each terrain type yields differing proportions of resources, so the type of terrain you choose for a city site determines the level of the city's success.

Our imaginary Settler happens to be on a Grassland square. Normally, Grassland produces two food when worked by one of your citizens. Some Grasslands have a small symbol in the center of the square (a rocky tuft). That means that these extra-fertile Grassland squares also yield one shield when worked (in addition to the normal output).

Forest squares, which produce only one food but two shields, also appear nearby. The Forest to the northwest of our imaginary starting point contains the village of a minor tribe; this can have many different ramifications for your civilization, which we will go into detail a little later on.

A couple of Coast squares are also nearby. The Coast terrain type produces one food and two income from commerce when worked by one of your citizens. Two of the Coast squares contain Fish (one of many special resources available), which provides three food and two commerce. The multiple Fish make this an excellent site for a city.

You have the option of moving around to find a suitable city site. If the nearby terrain is less than optimal, it is worth doing so, considering the importance of proper city placement. You shouldn't waste too much time looking, however. Settlers move only one square per turn, and many years pass every turn this early in the game. Luckily, our imagined starting position is excellent; the local terrain provides a diverse resource mix, we're adjacent to an ocean coast, and Grassland squares make good city locations.

We build our first city by clicking the Build City Orders button or pressing [B]. The suggested name is fine, so we end up with Washington.

## Examining the City Display

A newly built city has a population size of 1, so it's just a *town*. (It becomes a *city* when it grows to size 7.) As soon as the town is built, a new window called the City Display

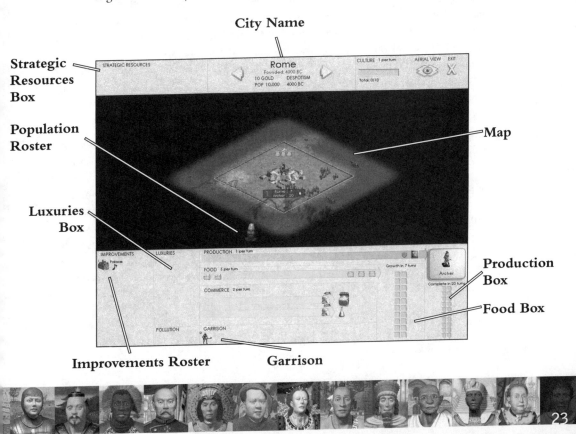

City Name

Strategic Resources Box

Population Roster

Luxuries Box

Improvements Roster

Garrison

Map

Production Box

Food Box

appears. It gives detailed information on the town's current status, including the amount of each thing produced, the item currently being built, and the size and attitude of the population. See **Chapter 15: Reference: Screen by Screen** for all the details.

Our first priority is to check the status of the town's resources. The Population Roster shows that the town of Washington has one citizen, and he is content. Under most circumstances, each citizen in a city is working in one of the surrounding terrain squares, generating resources for the city's use. As new citizens are added, they're put to work in the most productive terrain square available. In this case, the city's single resident is laboring in a Coast square that contains a Fish.

You have the option of moving citizens to different terrain squares if you want to produce different combinations of resources. In our situation, we can see by the icons on the map of the City Radius that the Fish square is generating three food and two coins. If we were to click that Fish square, the citizen working there would be taken off duty. We could then click on another square to assign this idle citizen to it.

The amount of each resource produced is based on terrain type. Under normal circumstances, each city can assign citizens to generate resources in any of the 20 surrounding terrain squares. Since this city is new, however, the workable radius is temporarily limited to the nearest eight. The pattern of 21 squares with the city at the center is called the City Radius. In addition to the terrain squares in the City Radius, the city square itself always generates resources. Like the squares worked by your citizens, the number and type of resources produced in the city square is dependent on the terrain type. (Some circumstances can deny you access to the resources in some of the squares in the City Radius. We discuss those in **Chapter 6: The Basics of Towns and Cities**.)

Our little town is currently generating five units of food. Each citizen requires two units of food each turn in order to survive, so we have a net excess of three. Excess food accumulates in the Food Storage Box. The more surplus food the city generates, the faster it grows. Washington is also generating two shields. Shields represent the raw materials and labor used for building new units and city improvements. The shields generated each turn go directly into the Production Box. Finally, the city is producing four coins, which represent income from taxes on commerce. These are divided to three purposes: supporting scientific research, creating entertainment for your citizens, and enriching your treasury. You control how much goes to each using the Science and Entertainment Sliders, which we cover elsewhere.

Before we leave the City Display, we have to mention the Improvements Roster. This lists all the city improvements and Wonders in the city. At the start of the game, our first city has only a Palace. The Palace denotes that Washington is our civilization's capital.

## Early Priorities

There's a lot of information to assimilate at the start of the game, and it can be hard to know what you should do first. To thrive, keep these five priorities in mind early in the game: defense, research, growth, exploration, and culture.

**Defense:** Top priority is defending our capital from potential enemies. Who knows who might be lurking in all that unexplored territory? We must build a military unit. When the town is founded, it almost always automatically begins to construct a defensive unit. The Production Box shows that Washington is building a *Warrior*.

**Research:** A portion of our per-turn income is used to research new civilization advances. These are new discoveries and technologies that allow us to build newer and better military units, city improvements, and Wonders of the World.

**Growth:** The surplus food generated by the town eventually leads to population growth. When the Food Storage Box is completely filled, a new citizen is added to the population (and the box is emptied). Steady city growth leads to increased productivity and the ability to expand our civilization by building Settlers and Workers to colonize and tame the wilderness.

**Exploration:** If you don't explore the dark areas of the map, you have no way of knowing what benefits and dangers are lurking there. By using spare units to explore the world, you can discover the villages of minor tribes (which might provide all sorts of benefits), good potential sites for new cities, and neighboring civilizations.

**Culture:** Eventually, you'll want to expand your city's sphere of influence. This is your national border, and resources within it are yours to exploit. When you can afford to, you should build city improvements that contribute to culture. A Palace is one of these, so you have a head start.

## Researching Civilization Advances

When we finish with Washington (for now) and close the City Display, the first turn ends. At the start of the next turn, we're prompted to choose the first civilization advance we want to research.

At the moment, our civilization has only minimal knowledge. We have the three basic skills that are always available at the start—Irrigation, Mining, and Roads—plus one or two that were granted (as happens in some games) for no cost. The bulk of your knowl-

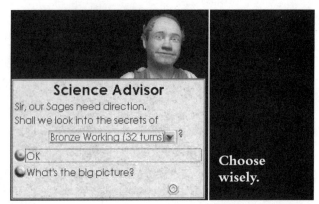

**Choose wisely.**

edge throughout the game is gained through research. Many different strategies are possible, each dictating the order in which you should research advances. For this game, we'll adopt a conservative, defensive strategy. You can experiment with research strategies of your own as you become more familiar with the game.

We ignore the Science Advisor's suggestion and click the arrow next to it. From the pull-down list, we choose *Bronze Working*. Why? The discovery of Bronze Working will allow us to build the Spearman unit. Spearmen are twice as effective at defending cities as Warriors.

The amount of time required to research a discovery is based on the amount of science our civilization (in this case, the one city) is generating. Remember, science funding is

**Our national research budget**

taken from tax income. We click on the Advisors icon, which opens the Domestic Advisor's report. We can see here that it will take five turns to discover Bronze Working. If that's too fast or (more likely) not fast enough, we can move the slider left or right to decrease or increase the percentage of our income allocated to science. (You can't allot more than 100%—no deficit spending!) If we budget too much to research, though, our treasury suffers.

Looking at the date, we see that several years of game time have passed. Early turns each span a number of years. As the game progresses, the turns get shorter, dropping eventually to one year apiece.

# Meanwhile, Back in the City...

Now, let's take a look at what happened in our town between turns. We double-click on Washington (on the map) to open the City Display. A few things have changed since we first looked. For one, the Food Storage Box is no longer empty. This is the surplus food that was generated on the first turn. It's stored here for later use. A note near the box tells us that it will be nine turns before enough food accumulates for the city to grow.

The Production Box is also no longer empty. The shields generated on the first turn were used to help build the Warrior. It's now only four turns from completion.

We press [Enter] to leave the City Display.

## First Military Unit

When the fifth turn rolls around, Washington has just built our first military unit. The Warrior is standing in the city square, with a marker flashing on and off around its feet. This means the unit is *active*—ready to receive orders.

You can do two things with a town's first military unit. You could use the unit to defend the city. In most cases, it is unwise to leave a city undefended. This is especially true if you know that an enemy unit is nearby. Early in the game, however, the world is sparsely populated, so you can take a chance and send the unit out to explore.

If you're at all curious, you probably want to see what that minor tribe to the northwest has in store for us. We could find another Warrior—or something better. However, since the results of encountering a minor tribe are unpredictable, the consequences might not be beneficial. We'll take the chance and move the Warrior to the northwest by pressing [7] on the numeric keypad (*not* the [7] on the top row of the keyboard). Note that when a unit moves next to a dark area, any black squares around it are revealed. Most units can "see" one square around them, unless they're on a hill or mountain. This is how you explore (and claim!) the neighboring terrain. At this point, our Warrior has not entered any unknown territory, so we can only see the same nine squares that we could at the beginning.

The turn ends automatically when our last unit finishes its movement. Since Warriors can move only one square per turn, our turn is now over.

## First Civilization Advance

We'll go back to exploring the world in a moment. For now, something interesting has happened. At the start of this turn, the Science Advisor announces that our researchers

have discovered the secret of Bronze Working. Excellent! We've discovered our first civilization advance.

When the message of discovery appears, you can click on the name of the advance to see the Civilopedia entry for your new technology. The Civilopedia is an in-game encyclopedia of game information. The entry for each advance shows (among other things) all the new units, improvements, and Wonders you can build as a result of the discovery.

It's once again time to choose a research project. The Science Advisor gives us his suggestion and the list of choices. This time, we'll select the Big Picture option. Our Science Advisor presents us with a detailed map of all the advances in the game. Using this "Tech Tree," we can explore possible future research paths and develop a long-term plan.

Bronze Working allows us to build Spearmen, and it allows research into Iron Working. Since Bronze Working has provided the ability to build a good defensive unit, we can move on to a research path that enhances our growth capability. We click on Pottery, and it's marked as *#1*, meaning that it's the first project in our Research Queue. (For the details on setting up a Research Queue, refer to **Chapter 9: Civilization**

**Advances** or the section on the "Science Advisor's Report" in **Chapter 15: Reference: Screen by Screen**.) We click Done to return to the map.

## Changing Production

Before we do anything else, it's time to check up on Washington again. We open the City Display and look at the Production Box. The city has automatically begun to build another Warrior. Unless you give it specific instructions, a city's governors will choose what to produce next by guessing at what you want. These guesses are based on the production orders you've given throughout the game—but this early in the game, there's no history of decisions for them to consult. Thus, they just go on blithely constructing whatever they think is best.

Since the city is still defenseless, we need to build a unit to protect Washington from possible invaders. A Spearman is a better defense than a Warrior, so we click on the Production Box to open the list of production options. Clicking on Spearman assigns that unit as the current construction project. The Spearman icon now appears inside the Production Box to indicate that the city is building one. We close the City Display.

## Finding a Minor Tribe

Remember our Warrior? The cursor is flashing under it again, indicating that it's once again ready for action. Our initial exploration (or starting point) revealed a village of huts to the northwest. This village, which the Warrior is now next to, is home to a minor tribe. Minor tribes are not rival civilizations (though some are home to barbarian raiders). They are small villages populated with people who might be inclined to help you.

We're about to make contact with this minor tribe. The results of such contact are unpredictable. It could result in a gift of knowledge or gold, the tribe might send their best warriors to form a military unit to help us, or the tribe might decide to join our civilization, either by ceding us their town or pulling up roots and forming a Settler. Of course, negative events are also possible; the village could be empty or populated by hostile barbarians.

We move the Warrior one square to the west, onto the hut, by pressing [4] on the numeric keypad. The result is good, but not great—we receive a gift of gold from the minor tribe. (A military unit would have speeded our exploration considerably.)

This early in the game, you're still paying nothing to support your units. The first several units are free of maintenance costs. How many? That depends on a few factors, including your form of government and number of cities. However, once you've built enough units, you'll begin paying support from your treasury on each one over the limit.

If you're over the limit and you receive a unit from a minor tribe, you have to support it, just as you support all your units. One coin from your commerce income goes to the upkeep of the new unit each turn. If this makes your units (as a whole) too expensive, you might consider disbanding the least useful of them. (The concept of disbanding is explained later.) On the other hand, if you capture a unit, it comes free of charge.

# Population Increase

We move the Warrior around for a few turns, exploring the area around Washington. Pretty soon, two things happen. First, the population of the town increases to two. Second, Washington completes the Spearman it was building. When we open Washington's City Display, we see that the Food Storage Box is now empty. Next turn, it will start filling up again, accumulating food for the next population increase.

The Population Roster now contains two citizens. On the map of the City Radius (the Resource Map), we can see that the new citizen is already at work; specifically, the citizen is producing two food and one shield in the Grassland-Shield square northeast of the city. That's fine for now. So, although we can change assignments if we choose, we'll leave the citizen there.

As for production, it's time to change again. This early in the game, one defensive unit is adequate for city protection. We click the icon of whatever the city has decided to build and select Settler from the Production menu. It's time to start thinking about the next priority: growth. In order to expand a civilization, you need to build other cities, and for that, you need Settlers. Here's a potential problem: when a city "builds" a Settler, it gives up *two* of its population to the emigration. We have to check the number of turns it'll take to complete the Settler against the number of turns before the town will grow to size 3. Luckily, the town will grow before the Settler is done, so there will be enough people to go around. Relieved, we close the City Display.

## Garrisoning

Now the Spearman unit is flashing. In order to protect the city, the Spearman must remain inside Washington. Units provide the best protection when they are garrisoned. We garrison the unit by clicking the Garrison Order button or by pressing [F]. Garrisoned units remain in their city until you manually reactivate them. For now, the Spearman should be left alone to guard Washington.

# The Waiting Game

Soon, our wise men discover Pottery. In addition to opening up a further research possibility (Mapmaking), Pottery allows us to build Granaries, which store half the food when a new citizen is produced in a city. This *city improvement* greatly speeds the growth of towns and cities.

Our goal now is to develop Monarchy. In order to do so, we must first research Warrior Code, Ceremonial Burial, Mysticism, and Polytheism. Monarchy is a more advanced form of government that helps to increase our productivity. It also makes possible the Hanging Gardens Wonder of the World, which helps improve the attitude of our entire population.

Now that we have a long-term research goal, we can use the Tech Tree's Queuing feature. We use the Big Picture option to open the Science Advisor's report. Rather than choosing Ceremonial Burial as the next advance to research, we click on Monarchy. The intervening advances are marked as #1 (Ceremonial Burial), #2 (Warrior Code), #3 (Mysticism), and #4 (Polytheism). Monarchy is #5. A click on the Done button, and we're in business.

We need to move forward a few turns now, so we'll just move our Warrior around to explore a bit. Soon enough, we're notified that Washington has completed the Settler it has been building. We choose the Zoom to Washington option in the notification box to open the City Display. Once there, we change production so that Washington is building a Granary.

Washington's population has dropped to one. That's because, as we mentioned earlier, Settlers represent citizens who leave the city in order to establish a new city. The population will soon increase again, so the town's reduction in size is only temporary. We close the City Display.

# Expanding the Empire

Now it's time to expand the empire. We move the Settler northwest one square, west one square, then southwest three squares. It now occupies a Grassland square near a lot of Forest. Pressing [B], we order the Settler to build a new town. Again, we could name the city anything we want, but we'll just leave the default name of New York.

## Important Caveat

Sending our Settler out on its own like this is dangerous. Settlers are unarmed and cannot defend themselves if attacked. Any enemy unit—or even a barbarian unit—that comes along can simply capture our Settler. If this is done by an ally, it is of course an act of war—but this early in the game, we have no diplomatic agreements with any other civilizations that might be nearby.

When you send out valuable non-military units, especially Settlers and Workers, you take a calculated risk if you choose not to protect them with military units.

When New York's City Display opens, we notice a few differences from Washington's when it was first built. Although New York is producing just as much food as Washington did, commerce, and therefore tax income, is significantly lower. That's because the only special resource to take advantage of within New York's City Radius is Wheat, which produces food and shields, but no commerce income.

Here's something to note: even though there is still some unexplored terrain nearby, once you have established the town, all the squares in the City Radius are illuminated. Although this is a handy way to find out what's in those dark squares, it can be a nasty surprise to find an enemy unit on the doorstep of a vulnerable new city.

The New Yorkers guessed that we wanted them to produce a Spearman. Since this city needs to be protected too, a Spearman is just what we want, so we close the City Display without making any changes.

When we're notified that we've discovered Ceremonial Burial, we simply approve the next project. (We'll do the same the next few times research choices roll around.)

In a few more turns, New York completes its Spearman. Next, we want the city to produce a Worker. The production of Workers, like Settlers, costs population—only one, though, rather than two. After making sure that the town will have at least a population

of 2 by the time the unit is completed, we change the production in New York to a Worker.

While we're waiting for the Worker, we can explore New York's hidden terrain to the west. We move the Spearman west, then march south and north, lighting all that dark terrain. Finally, we bring it back into New York and garrison it.

A few turns later, Washington completes its Granary. We change the production to another Worker (after another population check). We can use these Workers to improve the terrain around Washington and New York.

Somewhere along the line, we also discover an advance and start on Mysticism. This will make the Oracle Wonder possible, and maybe later we'll try to build it.

# Improving the Terrain

Soon, New York finishes building its Worker. We change production there to a Granary. When the Worker becomes active, we move it one square to the northwest (using [7] on the numeric keypad), onto the Grassland square. Next, we open New York's City Display.

When we look at New York's Resource Map, we see that the Grassland square northwest of the city is currently generating one shield and two food. That's not bad, but we can use our Worker to improve the production in that terrain square. We close the City Display and, when the Worker becomes active, click the Build Road Order button or press [R].

For the next couple of turns, the Worker works on building a road. When the Worker becomes active again, there's a road leading out of New York to the northwest. We open New York's City Display again and look at the Resource Map. After the construction of the road, the same Grassland square is now generating one commerce in addition to its former resources. Not only do we get this benefit, but roads also increase movement speed; friendly units move three times faster along a road, no matter what type of terrain the road passes through.

Even better, the terrain can be improved further. When the Worker becomes active again, we'll click the Build Irrigation Order button or press [I]. Building irrigation takes a bit longer than building roads. It's likely that while we're waiting for the Worker to complete this task, Washington will produce its Worker. We change production to Wealth in Washington. This will generate some extra cash. Then we send the Worker northeast to build a road and irrigation in that Grassland square.

We also discover Mysticism and start work on another civilization advance, Polytheism. Monarchy is next on the list.

Several turns later, the New York Worker completes the irrigation project; the terrain square is now marked to show that it is irrigated. We open the City Display for New York and note that the resource production has not changed as a result of irrigation. Normally, irrigation increases the food output of Grasslands by one. However, under Despotism, our current system of government, any terrain square producing three or more of any resource type has its production reduced by one. So, instead of three food, the square still produces only two. This illustrates one of the drawbacks of Despotism and explains why our research is now proceeding toward Monarchy, under which such penalties do not exist.

While we're waiting to discover Polytheism and then Monarchy, we send the New York Worker southwest into the Forest square and build a road. Then, we move south and build both a road and irrigation. When the Washington Worker finishes building both, we move it one square west and repeat the improvement process. Then, we build a road connecting Washington to New York.

Neither of our cities has any *luxuries* inside its City Radius, but if either one did, the road connecting the two would be much more than just a boon to travel. When any city is connected to a luxury—a special terrain resource (like Incense) that isn't linked to food, production, or commerce—that's inside your nation's borders, one content citizen of the city is made happy for each of these luxuries. If one of your cities has no luxuries of its own but is connected via road, harbor, or airport to a city that does, the full benefit of the luxuries applies to *both* cities. In fact, by connecting a number of cities and luxuries with a network of roads, you can share the luxuries (and the happiness benefits) throughout your empire.

When we finally discover Monarchy, Map Making becomes our next advance goal. Now, it's time to change governments. During this turn, we're offered the opportunity to start a revolution and change governments. We choose to do so. There will be a few turns of anarchy before our population settles down, so we'll digress just a little.

Having Monarchy allows us to build the Hanging Gardens Wonder, and when we get Map Making, we can construct the Lighthouse, each of which grants huge benefits to our growing civilization. While we will try to complete these soon, Wonders are big projects and we have smaller concerns at present. So, after the anarchy settles down and our Monarchy is firmly in control, New York eventually completes its Granary, and we change production to a military unit. We'll reassign Washington to start working on the Hanging Gardens.

## Changing Governments

By now, we have established a small but thriving civilization. We're doing well, but could do better. Here's how we'll improve our civilization by switching to a more advanced form of government.

Within a few turns (it's not always the same number), a menu appears listing the systems of government currently available to us. We choose Monarchy, and our civilization is now ruled as one.

**Government Types**

Select a new government type.

- Despotism
- Monarchy

Let's take a look at the effects of the government change. We'll open Washington's City Display and look at the production changes. The city's food production has increased by three. Note that the Grassland square we irrigated earlier is now generating three food instead of two. The rest of the extra food is coming from the city square itself and one of the Fish squares. Commerce income has also increased as a result of the change in government, which has the effect of increasing the amount of science. Shield generation has remained the same, because none of the terrain currently in use around Washington is capable of producing more than two shields. If you look at the City Display for New York, you'll notice similar increases in that city as well.

## Meeting Another Civilization

We decide to explore to the southwest with New York's new unit (*not* with the vulnerable Worker). Eventually, we meet our nearest neighbors, the Germans. Their capital city, Berlin, is located some distance away. As soon as we enter German territory and run into a German unit, their leader requests an audience with us.

Establishing effective communication with your neighbors is vital to success. Early in the game, you should take any reasonable actions to ensure that nearby civilizations enjoy your company. Not only does this keep your civilization reasonably safe from attack, it can also lead to profitable exchanges. You can see your opponent's attitude toward you when you make contact with one another. The attitudes of rival leaders are based on your past behavior when dealing with other civilizations. Since this is our first contact with any civilization, we expect the German leader to have a neutral and somewhat cautious attitude (though you never really know what attitude a newly met leader will have).

Unless we declare war ourselves, we'll come out of this encounter with an automatic peace treaty with the Germans, and possibly an exchange of knowledge (advances). We want to make friends at this stage in the game, so even though giving up technology is dangerous, it's also a sign of trust and of hope for a strong alliance.

After this encounter, we have (most likely) gained a friend (for now) and possibly profited by one or two civilization advances as a result of technology exchange with the Germans. Now that we've made contact, we can chat with them at any time by clicking the Diplomacy button on the Info Box and sending an emissary to the Germans, or by right-clicking any German unit. The Germans can also contact us at any time.

## Conclusion

So ends the beginner's lesson. You should now be familiar with many of the basic concepts. Remember, we've only scratched the surface when it comes to learning the game. Use the rest of this manual and the Civilopedia to help you with new concepts as you encounter them.

Have fun, and good luck! May your reign be long and fruitful!

# IF YOU'VE PLAYED BEFORE...

*"I know the situation. Just tell me what's changed."*

If you've played before, much of what's in the game will be familiar, but there is much that's different, in ways both obvious and subtle. This chapter summarizes the major changes, and it's meant for experienced players. If you're new to the game, some of it might not make sense right away.

## General

Here are a few broad changes that affect the game overall.

**Civilization-specific advantages:** Each civilization always had its own personality and way of doing things, but now they also have specific game advantages. Every tribe also has one unit that only its civilization can build. See **Chapter 3: Setting Up a Game** for a list.

**Orders buttons:** Most of the menus are gone. Many of their functions are now contained in the Advisors' screens, but all of the orders you might want to give to a unit are right there on the World Map—those round buttons near the bottom. The lower row are the standard orders (Disband, Wait, and so on). Orders appropriate to the active unit in its current situation are in the upper row. Just click the button (or use the shortcut key) to give the unit its orders.

**Culture:** Every city and every civilization now earns *culture points* for having Wonders and cultural improvements, like Temples and Libraries. A city's cultural value translates into the size of its *sphere of influence*. Your cities' combined spheres of cultural influence determine your national borders. For explanations of the creation and benefits of culture, see the relevant sections in **Chapter 11: Managing Your Cities** and **Chapter 12: Managing Your Empire**.

**Mouse cursor scroll:** Move your mouse cursor to any edge of the World Map, and your view will shift in that direction until you move the mouse away from the edge again or reach one of the poles. This is a handy way to see terrain that's just out of sight or to scan large areas. The arrow keys (*not* the numeric keypad arrows) also move the map, in increments.

**Barbarians have been revamped:** The details are in **Chapter 8: Units**, but here are the high points:

- Barbarians don't just spring up out of nowhere. Now, they originate from encampments and have names. Villages on the coast can spawn seagoing vessels.

- There are no barbarian leaders. To get their gold, seek out and invade the barbarian encampments.

- Barbarians do not capture undefended cities. Now, they just pillage the place and move on. They don't give you that polite warning, either.

# Units

Armed forces and other units are, while perhaps not the heart of a civilization, certainly the parts you spend the most time dealing with. There've been a lot of changes here.

**No more shields:** The familiar shields that every unit in the *Civilization II* game carried have been replaced. A vertical health bar now accompanies every unit in the game. The length of this colored bar indicates the overall health of the unit. The bar is separated into segments, each of which represents one hit point. Green still indicates a healthy unit, yellow still means the unit has been somewhat damaged, and red still marks a critically injured unit. In this game, the coloring on the unit's uniform denotes nationality. (You can change the way units are displayed using the preferences in the Game menu.)

**No home city:** Support for military units now comes directly from your civilization's treasury. Unhappiness due to military units in the field is also managed in a new way, called "war weariness." (For the details, see **Chapter 12: Managing Your Empire**.) These two changes, taken together, make the idea that each unit has a home city no longer relevant. When units in an ally's territory are returned after an "accidental" incursion, they simply return to the nearest square that's neutral or in your territory.

**Paying for support:** All units beyond those supported for free (as determined by government type and number and size of cities) require funds from your treasury for support—even Settlers. No unit requires shields or food for support.

**Upgrading:** When some units become obsolete, you can upgrade them. Move the unit into any city with a Barracks and press [U]. If it's possible to upgrade the unit and the city is capable of building the new unit, the job is done.

**Diplomats and Spies:** Diplomats and spies are no longer units that move around the map. Instead, diplomatic and espionage missions are initiated and carried out through embassies. Read **Chapter 13: Diplomacy and Trade** for more information.

**Caravans or Freight:** Caravans and freight are also no longer units to be moved around the map. Instead, trade occurs along trade networks comprised of roads, harbors, and airports. See **Chapter 13: Diplomacy and Trade** for the details.

**Settlers and Workers:** Settlers are now good for only two things: founding cities and adding to the population of existing ones. They no longer improve terrain. That's now the job of the Worker. A Worker can also add to the population of an existing city, but can't establish a new one. A Settler costs *two* population to build; a Worker costs only one. Each contributes the same number when adding to a city as they originally cost. Neither Settlers nor Workers need food for support, as Settlers did in previous versions. Like all other units, they're supported with funds from your treasury.

**Capture:** Enemy forces can now capture defenseless units, like Settlers, Workers, and artillery. If there's no defender nearby, any military unit (one with an attack factor) can take control of a unit that's incapable of defending itself. A captured Settler or Worker retains its nationality, but serves its new civilization as unquestioningly as it did its previous ruler. A captured Settler becomes two Workers, because founding a city with only foreign nationals is a bad idea.

**Firepower gone:** Combat has been improved so that the concept of firepower is no longer necessary. For details, check out **Chapter 8: Units**.

**Bombard ability:** Warships, bombers, fighters, and artillery units have the ability to bombard a target that's within their range. Bombardment counts as a unit's attack, and might damage defensive fortifications, harm units, or otherwise damage a city in the target square. For more details, see **Chapter 8: Units**.

**Leaders:** No one can build leaders; they arise from battles. Get the leader back to one of your cities, and you have two options (both of which consume the leader; it disappears):

- *Create an Army.* A leader in a city can become an Army. Essentially, an Army is a ground unit that can include (transport) other ground units. When grouped into an Army, these units have advantages in combat. For the details, see **Chapter 8: Units**.

- *Finish a great work.* When it arrives at a city that's in the midst of building a Wonder or city improvement, a leader can whip the population into a productivity frenzy, so that they finish the project in one turn.

**New Worker orders:** A number of new orders make common terrain improvement jobs, like building a road from one point to another, easier and more convenient. The details are in **Chapter 8: Units**, and there's a list at the end of **Chapter 15: Reference: Screen by Screen**.

# Terrain and Movement

We all know how important terrain is to successful civilization building. Here are the major changes—large and small.

**Natural resources:** Natural resources work in a completely different manner than in previous *Civilization* games. They're divided into three categories: bonus resources, luxuries, and strategic resources. That's right; luxuries are now counted among the terrain specials. Strategic resources are necessary to build some units, and both can be traded. For the details, read **Chapter 7: Terrain and Movement** and **Chapter 13: Diplomacy and Trade**.

**Fresh water limit on irrigation:** Until your civilization discovers Electricity, your Workers can only irrigate squares with access to *fresh* water: a river, a lake, or another irrigated square.

**Shields from clearing forests:** When a Worker finishes clearing a Forest square, this delivers a number of production shields to the nearest city. The forest still changes into a terrain type more suited to irrigation, too.

**Colonies:** To collect a strategic resource or luxury from a terrain square outside a city's sphere of influence (see "Culture" in **Chapter 11: Managing Your Cities** to find out what that is), you can have a Worker establish a colony on that square. For the details, see "Orders" in **Chapter 15: Reference: Screen by Screen**.

**Effects of rivers:** The effects of rivers on movement and combat have been changed a bit, as follows:

- *No fast movement: **Civilization II** allowed ground units moving along rivers to travel faster—as if moving on a road. This game offers no movement bonus for river travel. Rivers now run along the edges of squares, not through them.

- *Combat bonus:* If combat takes place across a river—the units are on different sides when the combat begins—the defender gets a bonus.

- *Movement cost:* Until you discover Engineering, your units do not enjoy the road bonus to movement when they cross a river.

**Altitude affects visibility:** Units on high ground can see farther than usual, and units on Mountains can see over Hills. In no case can any ground or naval unit see over a Mountain square.

**Disease:** Cities near Jungle and Flood Plain terrain squares suffer a chance of being beset by disease. Units in Jungles can also be killed by disease.

**Impassable terrain:** Certain terrain is impassable to certain types of units. This is terrain that those units cannot traverse, usually due to physical limitations. For example, wheeled units like Catapults and Cannons cannot travel across mountain squares unless someone has built a road through the range. If one of your units runs into a square of terrain that is impassable to that unit, you'll know because it won't move into the square when you order it to.

# Cities

Most experienced players agree that managing your cities is the most important aspect of success in the game. Maybe they're right, maybe not, but what's certain is that we've made some changes to the way it works.

**Trade is now commerce:** The money that each city brings in, which used to be called *trade*, is now *commerce*. Your net income per turn (after support and other costs have been subtracted) is divided between science funding and your treasury. Luxuries are also derived from terrain and trade.

**Production queue:** Now you can queue up your city's production. Just set up the city's production queue and then press [Shift]-[Q] to save it. When you want to load your saved queue, press [Q] to load it.

**Production suggestions:** When a city completes its current building project, it doesn't just start on another of the same thing. Rather, the city governors suggest what to build next, and that's what they start on unless you override them. Keep an eye on these guys. They learn from your choices in other cities, but they have their own agendas as well.

**City governors:** Every city has a group of bureaucrats who can help ease the burden of managing a large empire. See **Chapter 15: Reference: Screen by Screen** for the details.

**No penalty for changing projects:** The penalty for changing production in mid-project is gone—except for any shields lost as overrun.

**Wealth production:** "Wealth" is a project that has essentially the same effect as Capitalization—production converted into commerce income. The difference is that Wealth is available right from the start, with no technology prerequisite, but the income it generates is greatly reduced.

**War weariness:** When you continually wage war or remain on a war footing, your citizenry eventually get tired of it. This effect is known as war weariness. Under representative governments (Republic and Democracy), war weariness causes great unhappiness in your cities. For the details, see **Chapter 12: Managing Your Empire**.

**Wonders:** You'll find the list of Wonders of the World (and their effects) somewhat different. New to this game is the concept of *Small Wonders*. These are great projects that aren't necessarily one of a kind. For example, all civilizations can build their own Apollo Program now, instead of there being only one that delivers space flight to everybody. Check out **Chapter 10: Wonders** for more detail—and see the Civilopedia for descriptions of the new Wonder effects.

**City improvements:** What's true of the Wonders of the World is also true to a lesser extent of city improvements; the list of improvements and their effects have been improved. Though you'll find most of the possibilities familiar, there have been one or two changes. Check out the Civilopedia for the specifics.

**Conquest:** When you take over an enemy city, you have the option to raze it, rather than taking control of it. Also, cities of size 1 are not destroyed when you occupy them.

# Advances

The progress of science and the way you control it within the game have been significantly improved. For more information on any of the topics below, refer to **Chapter 9: Civilization Advances**.

**Advances tree:** Not only have many of the technologies had their effects changed, but there are new advances (and one or two old ones are gone). The tree is now diagrammed for you in the Science Advisor's screen, so go take a look.

**Ages:** The passage of history in the *Civilization* games has always been divided into ages, but now it's explicit. You don't have to discover every advance in an age to complete it, but you must complete most of them to move on to the next age.

**Research queue:** You can now set up a research schedule. On the Science Advisor's screen, you can choose a target technology and have the advances between here and there scheduled for you, or you can specifically determine the order in which every advance will be researched.

# Diplomacy

The way diplomacy works is different, but not so much so that you'll feel lost. The details are in **Chapter 13: Diplomacy and Trade**.

**Making contact:** You still generally make first contact with your opponents by running across their units, but now you can also trade with leaders you have already met to gain *communications* with those you haven't.

**Establishing embassies:** You still can't establish an embassy with another civilization until after you've discovered Writing, but now you *pay* to set up diplomatic relations (and a base for underhanded activities). An embassy also opens the possibility of diplomatic agreements beyond a simple peace treaty.

**Diplomatic missions:** Once you have an embassy with another nation, you can click the embassy icon (at their capital city) to open a menu of the possible diplomatic activities. These all cost gold to attempt.

**No Diplomats or Spies:** That's right, none. With the change in the way embassies are established and run, all the major functions of the Diplomat and Spy units have become redundant.

**Espionage:** After you've discovered Espionage and built the Intelligence Agency, your embassies can undertake espionage mission for you. See "Espionage" in **Chapter 13: Diplomacy and Trade** for the details.

**Expanded trading options:** You can still trade maps, lump sums of money, advances, and everything you could before. Now, you can also trade, receive, or demand diplomatic agreements, per-turn payments, communications with leaders, luxuries, strategic resources, Workers, and even *cities*.

**Trade agreements:** Trade routes and supply and demand have been integrated into diplomacy. If you want to set up ongoing commerce with another civilization, you must do it explicitly during negotiations. You and the other leaders can trade surplus resources and luxuries in any way you see fit. All trade agreements last 20 turns before coming up for review (unless war cuts them off).

**World Map and Territory Map:** You have a new option when trading maps with other leaders. You can still give or get the same World Map, which includes everything you've explored or been told about—including the locations of all your cities. The new option is the Territory Map, which gives only the outline of your borders (your cities' cultural spheres of influence).

# What's Gone

The experienced *Civilization* player will notice a few omissions. Some of these have already been mentioned, but because their effects on strategy are so broad, we thought they deserved repeating.

**Science and entertainment limits:** No matter what your form of government, the only limitation on your level of funding is what you can afford.

**Zones of control:** The idea that any unit can interdict the terrain squares that surround it has been discarded. This means that units of different nationalities can move freely around among each other. However, the idea that some military units can take advantage of their speed and the proximity of an enemy unit remains. These units can launch an attack on any enemy unit foolish enough to pass through an adjacent terrain square.

**Engineers:** As your technological know-how grows, your Workers will be able to put some discoveries to practical use—they gain new abilities. (Engineering and Electricity grant new skills to your Workers.) When your Workers excel at self-improvement, Engineers become unnecessary.

**Caravans and freight:** Trade is conducted differently in the *Civilization III* game than in previous versions. (For details on the new trade system, see **Chapter 13: Diplomacy and Trade**.) The new system makes units whose purpose was solely for trade purposes unnecessary, so they're not in the game. This raises a couple of questions:

- *Without them, how do you set up trade routes?* Trade routes have been revamped too. This is now a function of your trade network (roads, harbors, and airports) and diplomacy. You no longer need to send special units to do the job.

- *What about speeding up the production of large projects (i.e., Wonders)?* The only way to speed production of a Wonder is to use a leader. Stockpiling Caravans or Freight units around a city in preparation for building a Wonder in record time is no longer possible.

**Bribery:** Even though we mentioned it when discussing spies, it doesn't hurt to make things completely clear. You can no longer bribe enemy units. Your enemies cannot bribe your units. Clearly, this change will have a major effect on many players' strategies.

**Fundamentalism:** Government based on religious fanaticism is no longer an option.

**The Senate:** That's right. Republics and Democracies no longer have those pesky Senators refusing to let you go to war and forcing you into unwanted treaties. However, your citizens' war weariness affects your decisions in a similar way. For a discussion of war weariness, see **Chapter 12: Managing Your Empire**.

# THE BASICS OF TOWNS AND CITIES

*"There is no city of gold."*

When you start a game, your first units are surrounded by the darkness of the unknown. Though you could choose to let this Settler and others wander around, the first military unit they ran across would capture them. As soon as you find a decent site, you should have your Settler build a permanent settlement—a town. You must build at least one town, because only towns (which grow into cities and metropolises) can produce units, food, income from commerce, and all the other things that allow your civilization to grow and develop. You'll probably build a dozen or more towns over the course of the game.

## A Note on Terminology

Throughout this manual, we use the term "city" to refer to towns, cities, and metropolises. It's less awkward than repeating "towns, cities, and metropolises" all over the place. The exception, of course, is in cases when the size makes a difference.

Cities are the residences of your population, the sources of tax dollars and cultural development, and the homes of your scientists. Each city organizes the development of the area surrounding it, harvesting nearby agricultural produce, natural resources, and potential trade goods, then converting these resources into food, industrial production, technology, and cash.

One way to measure the success of your civilization is by the number and size of cities you control. Larger cities collect more taxes, conduct more scientific research, and produce new items faster. Civilizations with small numbers of cities and small city sizes risk being overrun by larger, more powerful neighbors.

You can acquire new cities in a few ways. Most frequently, you build them with Settlers. If you are aggressive, you can conquer the cities of your neighbors. Occasionally, your exploring units will discover a minor tribe that elects to join your civilization. If your culture is dominant, a neighboring, culturally weak city might be swayed by your city's cultural influences and spontaneously leave its civilization and convert to yours. Finally, there's propaganda; it's one of the less ethical tools of diplomacy, but it can be quite effective in bringing cities under your rule.

# The City Display

The primary tool you use to monitor and control your cities is the City Display. This display opens whenever you found or acquire a city, or you can double-click on any of your cities to open it. To comprehend the City Display, you must understand the symbolism it uses. Take a look at the City Display while you're reading—it'll make things a lot clearer.

Cities arose when populations banded together and began using planned agriculture to produce the food to feed themselves day to day. Often, there were sufficient leftovers to store for later use. Once food storage developed, not every citizen had to produce food all day, which allowed some people to specialize in producing other goods and services. Eventually, cities accumulated enough surplus food and goods that they could trade their excess with nearby populations.

To represent a city's population, the game maintains a Population Roster. Each citizen (a little head) stands for a segment of that city's population. The roster displays both citizens who labor on the land around the city and citizens whose specializations produce other effects. The Population Roster tells you how large your city has grown, who's happy and who's not, and the nationality of each citizen (you'll find lots more details

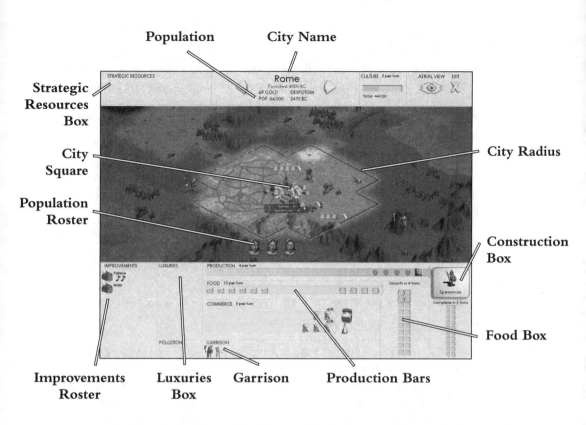

**Population** — City Name

**Strategic Resources Box**

**Rome**
Founded: 4000 BC
69 GOLD    DESPOTISM
POP 64,000   2470 BC

STRATEGIC RESOURCES

CULTURE  2 per turn

Total: 44/100

AERIAL VIEW    EXIT

**City Square**

**City Radius**

**Population Roster**

**Construction Box**

IMPROVEMENTS       LUXURIES       PRODUCTION  4 per turn

Palace
Walls

FOOD  10 per turn

COMMERCE  6 per turn

Growth in 4 turns

Spearman

Complete in 5 turns

POLLUTION       GARRISON

**Food Box**

**Improvements Roster**       **Luxuries Box**       **Garrison**       **Production Bars**

under "Population Roster" in **Chapter 15: Reference: Screen by Screen**). Since there are other points of interest in this display, we're moving on.

Citizens laboring on terrain squares (or "map squares") produce three different things: food, shields, and commerce. (Shields represent common raw materials and the labor the city uses to produce goods.) Some terrain produces a larger proportion of one than the others. On some squares, citizens can't produce any of one type (a citizen working on undeveloped Tundra produces no shields, for instance). Each square's production of food, shields, and commerce is shown on the City Display in a Resource Map, and the city's totals are summarized in the Resource Bars below it.

# Founding New Towns

The most common way you gain new cities is by sending out Settlers to build them and Workers to tame the wilderness around them. The terrain under and around your city is important, so if you want to select the best possible place for your future metropolis, make sure to read "Choosing Your Location" below. (If you want to jump right in, choose a square with rivers and special resources near it.)

When a Settler stands on the square where you wish to build a new town, press [B] or click the Build Order. (If you're not sure which button is which, just put your mouse cursor over each one until the identifying text appears.) If you choose Build by mistake, you can click the X icon on the Name City screen to call the whole thing off.

Your advisors propose a name for the new town; type in a different name if you prefer. When you're satisfied, press [Enter] or click the O icon. The City Display opens so that you can arrange the town's initial production and economic development. The Settler disappears; it becomes the first citizens of your new burg.

## Choosing Your Location

Choose the sites where you build towns carefully. Citizens will work the terrain surrounding the city square in an X-shaped pattern (see "City Radius" below for a diagram showing the exact dimensions). This area is called the City Radius. The terrain square on which the Settler was standing becomes the City Square. The natural resources available where a population settles affect its ability to produce food, shields, and commerce. Cities near fresh water sources can irrigate to increase crop yields, and cities near mineral outcroppings can mine for raw materials. On the other hand, the arid terrain will always handicap cities surrounded by desert, and cities encircled by mountains find arable cropland at a premium.

In addition to the economic potential within the city's radius, you need to consider the proximity of other cities and the strategic value of a location. Ideally, you want to locate cities in areas that offer a combination of benefits: food for population growth, raw materials for production, decent income, and natural resources.

## Natural Resources

When you look around your world, you're sure to notice the icons that appear on some terrain but not on most. Each of these represents natural resources that exist in

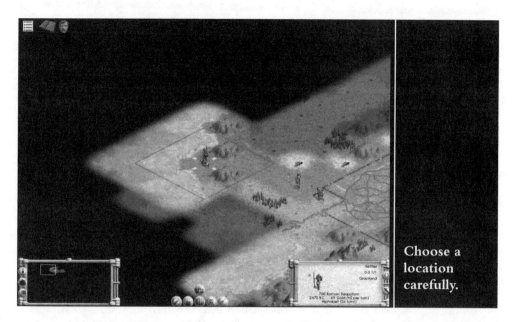

**Choose a location carefully.**

abundance in that area. These resources are divided into three categories, according to their uses:

- **Bonus resources** are those resources that increase the productivity of your city. A vein of Gold, for example, can increase the amount of commerce income a city generates. The presence of Wheat raises the food production potential.

- **Luxury resources** are resources you can use to keep your citizens happy. As your civilization grows, discontent can become a serious problem. Luxuries—things like Silk, Dyes, and Wine—help keep your people satisfied that you're ruling well. (For the details on keeping your citizens happy, read "Happiness and Civil Disorder" in **Chapter 11: Managing Your Cities**.)

- **Strategic resources** are materials necessary for building certain units, improvements, and Wonders. If you have no Iron, for example, you can't build armor for Knights or rails for Railroads. As your civilization advances, you'll become aware of new strategic resources that you were unable to appreciate earlier. Strategic resources are more likely to appear on certain terrain types, so it's not impossible to predict where these might appear.

When possible, you should locate your cities to take advantage of these resources. See **Chapter 7: Terrain and Movement** for more details and a discussion of the resources' benefits.

## Proximity of Cities

A serious consideration when planning new cities is the current or potential location of other cities. You want to minimize the chance that one city's radius overlaps another's. Since a map square can only be used by one city at a time, radius overlap restricts the potential growth of one or both cities. Explore nearby lands as soon as possible to begin planning the placement of future cities.

## Strategic Value

The strategic value of a city site is a final—but vital—consideration. A city square's underlying terrain can increase the city's defensive strength when it comes under attack. In some circumstances, the defensive value of a particular city's terrain might be more important than the economic value. Good defensive terrain (Hills, for example) is generally poor for food production and inhibits the early growth of a city, but can be a valuable military asset. You'll have to do a little extra to get these cities to grow and prosper. Regardless of where a city is built, the city square is easier to defend than the same unimproved terrain.

The larger a settlement's population, the better the innate defense it provides to military units stationed there. In a town you can build Walls, which increases this defense factor to equal those of units in a city of size 7. (Walls have no effect on defense factors in a city of size 7 or above.)

Placing some cities on the seacoast gives you access to the ocean. You can launch ships to explore the world and to transport your units overseas. You can build Harbors to enlarge your trade network to include other continents. (Trade networks are discussed in **Chapter 13: Diplomacy and Trade**.) With few or no coastal cities, your sea power and commercial potential are limited.

**Walls help keep out the riff-raff.**

# Capturing Cities

Other civilizations normally defend their cities with one or more military units, and sometimes with Walls and other city improvements. You can identify a defended city, because when you approach, the best defending unit is plainly visible. You can tell a walled city by the short wall surrounding it. There are three ways to acquire enemy cities: force, defection, and subversion. Defection happens without any immediate action on your part, but the others require an active hand.

If you choose force, you must destroy the defenders by successfully attacking with your military units. Once the city is undefended, you can move in and capture it. If you prefer subversion, you must successfully sow propaganda in the city. (This requires a planted spy and a significant outlay of funds.) Dissident citizens capture the city for you. You can't directly cause a defection, but you encourage it by building up your cities' cultural strength. When a rival city is near your borders and your culture vastly outranks theirs, a strong desire to enjoy the benefits of your society can drive the citizens to defect and join your empire.

If captured by military means, a city becomes yours to raze or to keep. If you let it stand, you install new governors to control and manage as you instruct.

Acquiring an enemy city can also lead to side benefits, such as plundered gold and captured Workers.

Capture does not affect Wonders of the World, but destroying a city does (see **Chapter 10: Wonders** for more details). Small Wonders in a city are always destroyed when the city changes hands.

# Converting Minor Tribes

As your units explore the world, they might encounter minor tribes—civilizations too small or nomadic to count as "settled" (see "Minor Tribes and Barbarians" in **Chapter 7: Terrain and Movement** for the scoop on these situations). Minor tribes react to contact with a range of emotions, from delight to hostility. Occasionally, a minor tribe is sufficiently awed by your emissaries to immediately form a new city and become part of your civilization.

Feeling
lucky?

Move your exploring unit onto the minor tribe's huts to discover the tribe's attitude toward your civilization. If they choose to form a new city, you need do nothing. Your advisors propose a name for the new city (which you can change).

## Renaming Your City

You can rename any of your cities whenever you wish. This is useful if you want a captured city's name to be consistent with the names of cities you have founded.

On the Map screen, simply right-click on the city and select Rename from the mini-menu. A dialog box opens in which you can type in the new city name. Press [Enter] or click the O icon to accept the name. If you decide not to change it, click the X icon.

## The Parts of a City

Cities can be viewed in three different ways: the city square, the city radius, and its cultural influence.

## The City Square

The terrain a city occupies is especially important, because it is always being worked. You cannot take the workforce off this square when moving citizens around on the City Display.

## The City Radius

The potential area of development, called the City Radius, extends out from a city in an area three map squares wide—two squares to the northeast, northwest, southwest, and southeast. The resulting "radius" looks like a fat X. The citizens of the city can work any square in this radius if it's within the city's borders to produce food, commerce, and shields. If the population gets large enough, you could have them working the entire area.

For the city's population to survive and grow, the radius must encompass terrain that the citizenry can cultivate to produce food. Grasslands and Plains are naturally the most fecund, and you can increase the agricultural output of most terrain types with irrigation.

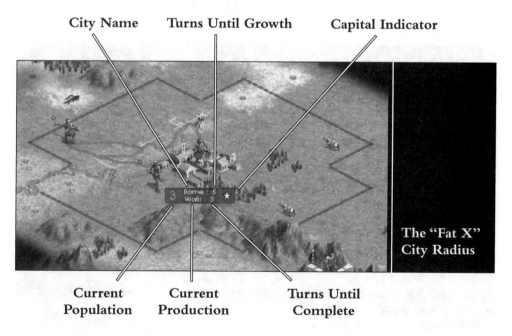

City Name    Turns Until Growth    Capital Indicator

The "Fat X" City Radius

Current Population    Current Production    Turns Until Complete

Your most important cities also have raw materials (shields) available. Forests naturally produce a number of shields, and Hills and Mountains can be mined to produce good quantities of raw materials. Some special natural resources—Cattle and Whales, for example—increase the shield production of a square, as do most strategic resources (see "Special Natural Resources" in **Chapter 7: Terrain and Movement** for complete details).

The importance of commerce (and the resultant taxes) in generating income and the funding for researching civilization advances can also make a location an especially good site for a city. Rivers, lakes, and coastlines are naturally rich in commercial potential. You can even generate commercial income from squares that naturally produce none, if you build roads to encourage trade.

If a square within your City Radius is outlined, it is being used by—and benefiting—another city. If you own both cities, you can flip between City Displays to adjust production in each to the best benefit of both locations.

## Cultural Influence

Every city is a population center, a military base, and a source of income. A city is also a center of *culture*. Every city has a cultural influence on the surrounding countryside,

Large cultural influences often overlap.

represented on the map by borders. As time goes on and you build improvements in a city, its influence grows and the borders expand. We go into more detail about culture in **Chapter 11: Managing Your Cities**.

When another civilization's unit is within your cultural borders, it is trespassing in your territory—unless you have agreed to allow that civilization right of passage. (See **Chapter 13: Diplomacy and Trade** for an explanation of that.) You can contact the owner of the stray unit and demand that it be immediately withdrawn. Right-click on the offending unit to do so.

# TERRAIN AND MOVEMENT

*"We do not inherit the land from our ancestors; we take it from those who defend it poorly."*

## Terrain and Movement Concepts

As mentioned in "City Concepts" in the previous chapter, the game map is divided into small squares, each containing a distinct type of terrain. These are called *terrain squares*. To represent that some terrain is easy to walk across and some requires slogging through mud or hacking through thick underbrush, your units spend *movement points* to enter each new square. Every unit has an ADM rating; the acronym stands for Attack/Defense/Movement. The third number in the rating (M) indicates how many movement points it can spend in a turn. You can find out all about units and their ADM ratings under "Unit Concepts" in **Chapter 8: Units.**

Each terrain type has its own *movement point cost.* Your Workers can lower these movement point costs by improving terrain (see "Settlers and Workers" in the next chapter). When a unit moves into a new square, it pays that square's movement point cost. If it has any movement points (or fractions thereof) left after moving one square, a unit can move again until it runs out of movement points. Since an attacking unit moves into the square vacated by a defeated defender, your units also spend movement points to attack.

The proximity of enemy units or cities can also restrict a unit's movement options. For one thing, your units cannot share a square with either. Less obvious is the fact that some units can attack your units as they pass. This can also restrict a unit's movement options. (For more detail, read "Retreat" in **Chapter 8: Units**.)

Experienced players should note that only certain military units have *zones of control*, and that they work differently (free attack instead of movement limitation).

Your units will occasionally encounter terrain that is *impassable* (the unit simply does not move when you order it to). This is terrain that the unit in question cannot enter. For example, wheeled units require a road to travel through Jungles and Mountains.

## Types of Terrain

Each type of terrain has its own economic usefulness, effect on movement, and effect on combat. Detailed information about the terrain types is provided on the Map screen, in the Civilopedia, and in the **Appendix**.

To get terrain information on the Map screen, right-click on the square in question. A pop-up box shows you everything you need to know about the terrain. (If you don't recognize the icon for a special resource, this is the quickest way to identify it.) To look up a terrain type in the Civilopedia, click on the Civilopedia icon (the book) and select the Terrain option. A list of all standard terrain types appears.

Grassland — Food: 2 Shields: 1 Gold: 0

### About Rivers

The presence of a river adjacent to a terrain square indicates access to fresh water for irrigation (assuming the terrain can be irrigated). You cannot irrigate without fresh water (rivers or lakes) until your tribe discovers Electricity.

Rivers convey a commerce bonus to squares near which they run, in addition to the yield of the basic terrain. When any unit moving on a road crosses a river, it loses the road's movement benefit. This is true until your civilization discovers Engineering. If combat takes place across a river—the units are on different sides when the combat begins—the defender gets a bonus.

## Standard Terrain Types

The standard types of terrain can be divided along climactic lines. Below is a brief summary:

- **Tundra** is cold terrain. It doesn't produce much in the way of raw materials and can't be converted into more profitable terrain.

- **Jungle** and **Flood Plains** are wet terrain. Jungles are difficult to move through, and it costs a considerable investment of time to convert either type into more profitable terrain. Units fortified and citizens laboring in Jungles have a chance of falling prey to disease. Flood Plains cannot be converted into any other type of terrain.

- **Plains** and **Grassland** squares are open terrain. Both are easy to travel across, and when irrigated, both produce substantial amounts of food.

- **Hills** and **Mountains** squares are both vertically challenging. They take some effort to travel across, but while you're up there, you get quite a view—two squares instead of one in all directions (except past mountains). These types of terrain yield more raw materials when developed by mining.

- **Coast**, **Sea**, and **Ocean** squares generate substantial amounts of commerce income, and cities on the coast can build seagoing units, Harbors, and other useful improvements.

- **Desert** squares are dry terrain that can be developed for marginal production.

- **Forest** squares are difficult to travel through, but yield decent raw materials. They can also be cleared to gain a one-time shield bonus.

## Natural Resources

Most standard terrain types have at least one natural resource associated with them. (Some terrain types have several.) Natural resources are represented by icons resting on top of the basic terrain square. Resources add significantly to the economic value of the terrain. Citizen laborers from a city can *work* a square inside the City Radius and gain the general benefits of a resource.

Over and above the boost to a city's production, however, certain natural resources are *strategic*—necessary for building certain units, improvements, or Wonders. (For example, without access to Horses, you can't train Horsemen.) A city doesn't need to have citizens working a square to gain this benefit; it simply must be connected to it.

A city gains access to a natural resource by being *connected* to it. Connection can be made in several ways. The most dependable is to have the resource inside your civilization's borders and a road from the resource to the city.

Other ways to gain access include:

- Having a Harbor on the same sea as another friendly city that also has a Harbor and access to the resource.

- Having an Airport in both this city and another friendly city that has an Airport and access to the resource.

- Having a colony on the resource and an unbroken road (or railroad) between the colony and the city.

- Trading with another civilization to gain a resource that they have access to. Your capital cities must be connected to one another before you can trade resources. (This, of course, is generally the least dependable method.)

Natural resources fall into three broad categories: *bonus resources*, *luxury resources*, and *strategic resources*. Bonus resources, like Game, Wheat, and Gold, simply contribute to the productivity of the city or your civilization as a whole. Luxury resources help you keep your population happy. Strategic resources, as mentioned earlier, are necessary for certain building projects. Tradable luxuries and strategic resources appear on the Diplomacy screen as potential items of trade. This is how you arrange to have another civilization provide you with a resource, as mentioned above. Since it takes only one square's worth of a resource to supply your entire civilization, any surplus from additional sources is available for trading purposes.

Here's a brief summary of the natural resources you might find. Note that many of these will not be visible at the beginning of the game. As your technology progresses, you'll become able to recognize strategic resources that were useless to you before.

# Bonus Resources

Bonus resources include Gold, which supplies your treasury with extra commerce every turn, and these others, all of which increase the food output of the square where they're found: Wheat, Cattle, Fish, Game, and Whales.

# Strategic Resources

The list of strategic resources is slightly longer:

- **Iron** is an important component of armor and edged weapons.

- **Horses** are one of the earliest forms of transportation, and mounted units have definite advantages over infantry.

- **Saltpeter** is necessary for the development of gunpowder.

- **Coal** is an easily harnessed (though often dirty) source of energy. Early methods of generating steam power rely on coal burning.

- **Oil** fills too many purposes in the modern economy to name. Though its pollution potential is problematic, most civilizations are willing to take the risks to gain oil's economic and industrial benefits.

- **Rubber**, like oil, has a marvelous abundance of uses in an industrial society. Among others, rubber gaskets, tires, and windshield wiper blades are vital parts in many vehicles, including military ones.

- **Aluminum** is an irreplaceable ingredient in most modern lightweight alloys.

- **Uranium** is essential to early methods of generating nuclear energy.

# Luxuries

Mollifying your irritable population with luxuries is no simple matter. Luxuries are something you must find and gain access to, like strategic resources. A city's access to luxuries works in exactly the same way as it does for strategic resources, making the methods of connection (roads, railroads, Harbors, etc.) even more valuable.

All of the luxuries a city has access to appear in the City Display. Each type makes one content citizen happy or (if there are no content citizens) one unhappy citizen content.

The luxuries that might be available to your civilization include Incense, Dye, Wine, Fur, Spice, Silk, Diamonds, and Ivory.

## Impassable Terrain

Impassable terrain is land that some types of unit cannot traverse, usually due to physical limitations. For example, Catapults and Cannons cannot travel across mountain squares unless someone has built a road through the range.

## Terrain Improvement

When surveying sites for a new city, remember that terrain can be improved. Hill and Mountain squares can be mined to produce more raw materials. Plains and Grassland can be irrigated to produce more food. Jungle squares can be cleared to yield Grassland. Forest can be cleared to yield Plains. Plains and Grassland squares can be timbered to yield Forest if you need raw materials.

Workers can also improve terrain by building roads to increase the commercial value of the terrain. All terrain types produce commerce once penetrated by roads. Railroads further lower the movement point cost of the terrain across which they are laid, and they increase production as well. For more information on terrain improvements, see "Settlers and Workers" in **Chapter 8: Units**—Workers are the units that do the work.

## Disease

Cities in Flood Plains and units and cities in Jungles risk death by disease.

## Planetary Caretaking

Manipulating terrain to produce more shields has a downside, of course. One cost of heedless industrial growth is pollution and poisoning of the environment. Of the many dangers posed by pollution, the one most important to your civilization is the loss of a polluted square's productivity. Poisoning can also occur if nuclear weapons are detonated or a nuclear reactor melts down.

Pollution from industry and nuclear disaster are modeled as a balancing factor for growth. As you steer your civilization into the industrial age, you must manage your cities and monitor your terrain to minimize pollution.

# Pollution

Pollution appears within the City Radius of any city that is excessively productive (produces lots of shields) or has a very large population.

Pollution warning symbols begin appearing on the City Display when the combined pressures of smog and industrial pollution begin to create a significant threat of contamination. The number of symbols corresponds to the probability each turn of a square within the city radius becoming polluted.

Certain city improvements can help alleviate the situation. The Recycling Center reduces the impact of industrial pollution, in turn decreasing the accumulation of warnings. The Hoover Dam, a modern Wonder, acts as a Hydro Power Plant for all friendly cities on the same continent. The Mass Transit improvement minimizes smog.

A polluted square

## Special Contamination

The detonation of nuclear weapons or a disaster in a Nuclear Power Plant (a meltdown) also causes contamination.

## Nuclear Weapons

Nuclear units not only destroy the army or city they target, but all units stacked with the target and those in adjacent squares as well. The detonation also pollutes and devastates a number of map squares around the impact square. Your rivals might not spend the time or manpower to clean it up, but if you ever intend to use those squares, you should consider it.

## Nuclear Meltdown

If a Nuclear Power Plant suffers a catastrophic failure, half of the city's population is destroyed. Additionally, a number of squares near the city become polluted.

The risk of meltdown always exists when a city that has a Nuclear Plant goes into civil disorder. (Read "Happiness and Civil Disorder" in **Chapter 11: Managing Your Cities** for an explanation of civil disorder.) Civilian unrest might result in safety procedures becoming so lax that a catastrophic accident occurs. If you build this improvement in any of your cities, take special care not to allow those cities to go into disorder.

# Pollution's Effects

Pollution is represented graphically on the terrain square in which it occurs. It reduces the production of food, raw materials, and commerce income to zero. Once the terrain is detoxified, production returns to pre-pollution levels. Any Worker can detoxify polluted terrain. To order this, click the Clean Up Pollution order or press [Shift]-[C]. After a few turns of work, the pollution disappears.

# Monitoring Pollution

You're informed immediately when any map square within your territory becomes polluted, and the pollution appears on the map.

# Minor Tribes and Barbarians

Villages of thatch-roofed huts scattered about the map indicate the presence of minor tribes. These populations are too isolated, not organized enough, or too migratory to develop into major civilizations. Minor tribes come in two flavors: active and passive.

*Active* tribes are warlike groups that periodically send out raiding parties. Their warriors attack on sight and attempt to loot your towns and cities. If you find and obliterate an active tribe's village, you end the threat from that tribe (and get a bit of spare change in the process).

### Note to Experienced *Civilization* Players

Active tribes, as you might have figured out by now, are the new, *Civilization III* version of the barbarians encountered in earlier versions of the *Civilization* game. The village takes the place of the barbarian leader.

Though you might conquer the active tribes in your immediate area, new ones arise in areas that are outside your cultural borders, in areas that are not currently seen. As time passes, they appear at even farther distances from civilization. Thus, expanding your network of cities over a continent eventually removes the threat of active tribes, because the entire area has become more or less civilized by your urban presence.

*Passive* minor tribes react with a range of emotions to contact with your civilization. There is no way to predict any particular village's response, but most of the possibilities are favorable.

Here's what can happen when you move a unit into the village of a passive tribe:

The village of a minor tribe

- Occasionally the tribe is sufficiently advanced, yet awed by your emissary, to immediately form a new town and become part of your civilization.

- On the other hand, your troops might stumble on a village with an advance unknown to your civilization. Graciously, they share their knowledge.

- A village might have access to gold. To placate your emissary, they might offer some as a gift.

- The tribe gathers their fiercest young warriors together to create a military unit to join your civilization's forces—as a gesture of alliance (and perhaps a way to be rid of some young troublemakers).

- Your emissary makes a horrible faux pas, and the minor tribe turns vicious. A number of hostile units come boiling out of the village to attack.

- Your emissary arrives at a spot rumored to contain a village only to find the inhabitants long gone and the dwellings empty. Nothing occurs.

- Your unit catches up with a particularly nomadic tribe and impresses them with his or her goods and possessions. The minor tribe is willing to join your civilization, though not necessarily interested in settling in their present location. The villagers become a Settler.

- The minor tribe hands over a map of the surrounding area.

# Movement

### The Active Unit

How do you know whose turn it is to move? Every turn, the game activates each unit in turn by marking it with a blinking cursor. (If the new active unit isn't currently onscreen, the map centers on it, too.) You can give orders to each unit as it becomes the active unit (see "Orders" in **Chapter 15: Reference: Screen by Screen**).

If the active unit is difficult to see because it's on the periphery of your view, or perhaps partially covered by something else (the World Map, for example), press the Center key ([C]) to center the view on that unit.

There are two basic methods of moving units a square or two at a time: by keyboard commands or using the mouse. The keyboard method uses eight keys of the numeric keypad. The "5" key in the center is inactive; think of it as your unit's position. The keys surrounding the "5" represent the points of a compass. For example, pressing [7] sends your unit northwest, while pressing [6] sends your unit east.

The mouse method involves placing your mouse cursor on the unit, then clicking and dragging in the direction you want it to travel. The cursor turns into a square highlighting the unit's potential destination, with a path leading there from the unit's current position and a number noting how many turns it will take the unit to make the trip. Release the mouse button to assign the path and make the unit move. (This is an alternative version—best suited to short paths—of the GoTo order that you use to send a unit over long distances.) You can also select a destination square, then click and hold on that square. This assigns the active unit to go to that spot.

Units can move up to the limit of their movement allowance, with a few caveats. The most important exception is that a unit can always move at least one square in a turn, regardless of the movement point cost of the terrain.

A unit with a movement allowance greater than one must compare that with the movement point cost of the terrain square you wish it to enter. The unit pays the movement point cost (subtracts the cost from its remaining allowance) for each new square it enters, until you choose to stop moving or the unit's movement allowance is used up. When a unit is unable to complete a movement order because it doesn't have any points, its movement is finished for the turn. The game then activates the next unit.

Roads and railroads speed the movement of ground units. They do this by reducing the movement point cost of the terrain. Any terrain square with a road across it costs one-third of a movement point to cross. Any terrain square with a railroad costs nothing at all to cross. Cities automatically have roads in their city squares, so entering a city square from a square with a road always costs one-third of a movement point. Once your civilization discovers Steam Power, city squares are automatically upgraded to railroads too.

Explorers have the ability and equipment to move quickly through even the most difficult terrain. In game terms, they *treat all terrain as roads*. This means that it normally costs them only one-third of a movement point to enter any type of terrain—regardless of the actual existence of roads. Explorers can still use railroads for faster movement.

Sailing experience accumulates with new advances. In the early days, your Galleys have a 50% chance of being lost if they end their move in a Sea or Ocean square. Once your civilization can build Caravels, however, your crews are better trained. Caravels are never lost in Sea squares, but founder 50% percent of the time in Ocean squares. The more modern your navy, the less chance of losing them at sea.

# Special Orders

There are five special movement orders that deserve fuller explanations.

## Hold

If you want a unit to hold its position for the turn, press the Spacebar or click the Hold Order.

## GoTo Orders

To send a unit on a long trek, you have three options:

1. Click the GoTo Order (or use the shortcut key of [G]), then move your mouse cursor to the destination square and click there.

2. Click–and–hold on the unit, then (still holding) drag the cursor to the selected destination.

3. Find the destination square, then just click–and–hold on it until you see the GoTo path marker appear.

If the objective square you have in mind isn't currently visible on screen, you can Zoom Out (press [Z]) to enlarge the area you are viewing, click on the World Map to shift your view to another area of the map, or move your cursor to the edge of the screen to scroll the map in the direction you choose.

Once you've established a destination, the unit automatically goes to that square, whether it takes only one turn or many to complete its orders. If the unit is attacked or an obstruction prevents it from moving toward its goal, the unit becomes active again. Ground units cannot travel between continents on a GoTo order.

## Wait Orders

To skip a unit temporarily, press the Wait key ([W] or [Tab]) or click the Wait Order. This passes you on to the next unit and sends the skipped one to the end of the line. You'll see this unit activated again after all the others have had a chance to move.

## Airdrop Orders

Paratroopers that have not moved this turn have the special ability to make airdrops when in a city. Helicopters in a city can airdrop two ground units from that city. Press the Airdrop key ([A]) or click the Airdrop order. Your cursor turns into a parachute. You can make an airdrop into any visible land square within airdrop range of the origination square. If the target square is occupied by enemy troops, your dropped units will be killed. As you run the mouse over the map, the cursor changes from a parachute to a crossed-out parachute to indicate unsuitable destination squares. Click on a square to make the drop. Units that move by airdrop have no movement left after they drop.

## Airlift Orders

Once your civilization has discovered the requisite advance, you can build Airport improvements in your cities. Once you have two or more of these, you can airlift one unit with the Airlift ability per turn out of each. Activate a unit in a city, then click the Airlift order. A list of the cities with Airports appears, and you can select the unit's destination.

## Fortified Units

Units can be *fortified* on a square or *garrisoned* in a city. You can order a unit to stay in one place, usually for defensive purposes, by clicking the Fortify/Garrison order or pressing [F]. The unit will stay where you've put it until you activate it or it is attacked.

Fortified and garrisoned units do not automatically become active. If you want them to move, you must activate them yourself. If the unit stands alone, just click on it to activate it. Otherwise, right-click on the square in which it stands (or the ship). This opens a box listing all the units in that square. Click the name of the unit you wish to activate. Fortified units within a city can be activated by right-clicking on the city or from within the City Display—see "City Display" in **Chapter 15: Reference: Screen by Screen** for instructions on how to do this.

# Navigating the Map Window

We've talked about moving your units around the map, but several tools allow you to look at different map areas and move around the game world.

- You can simply click on a map square to center your view there.

- If you want to see a lot more territory, you can use the Zoom button [Z] to toggle to a wider view. This is a fully functional view; you can even play an entire game like this. Pressing [Z] again returns you to the default view.

- You can click on the World Map to move your view to an area you choose.

- Move the mouse cursor to any edge of the screen to start the map scrolling in that direction. To stop, just move the cursor away from the edge.

If the active unit is difficult to see because it's on the periphery of your view, or perhaps partially covered by something else (the World Map, for example), press the Center key ([C]) to center the view on that unit.

# Movement Restrictions

Most of the restrictions placed on unit movement are a matter of common sense, as we mentioned earlier. We're spelling them all out here, in case you try to order a unit somewhere that seems possible and the game won't let you do it.

## Ground Units

Ground units (all non-ship and non-air units) normally move only on land. They can cross rivers easily enough, but to traverse the wide (or narrow) oceans or even to get across lakes, they must board naval transport. In addition, some units find rough terrain impassable.

### Loading and Unloading

You can have a ship wait until it is loaded to capacity with units by clicking the Load order or pressing [L]. Boarding a ship uses up all a unit's movement points for the turn.

If you attempt to move a naval unit into a land square that does not contain a port city, any passengers who have not already moved this turn are offered the option to disembark and make landfall. You can also order a ship to unload all its passengers by clicking the Unload order or pressing [L].

## Impassable Terrain

As we mentioned earlier in this chapter, some units are prevented by their construction, weight, ungainliness, or other factors from moving across certain types of terrain. To these units, the terrain in question is impassable. The example you're most likely to encounter early in a game is Catapults; they can't travel into any Mountain or Jungle squares unless they're moving on a road.

# Naval Units

Ships normally move only on the ocean, although they can also sail across inland lakes. Ships cannot navigate any ground terrain in the game, including rivers, deltas, and flood plains. City squares that touch a shoreline along one side or at one corner are the only "land" squares that ships can enter—here they make port.

# Air Units

Air units do not have or use movement points like other units. Instead, each type has an *operational range*. This range is not affected by terrain type; air units can cross both land and sea squares. When you give an air unit a mission, the target of the mission must be inside the unit's operational range—it cannot fly any farther. Air units on air superiority missions have a *defensive range*, which is half of their operational range.

# UNITS

*"Give me a hundred fierce and loyal warriors, and I will bring peace from horizon to horizon."*

Units are groups of citizens and soldiers that can move around the world and interact with other units and civilizations. Some non-combat units—such as Workers, Scouts, and Settlers—have special functions that are explained separately.

## Unit Concepts

Each civilization's units have coloring that reflects whose service they are currently in. Units with white coloring are always barbarians.

Units can be divided into three types, according to the way they move: ground (or land) units, air units, and naval (or sea) units. Each unit has statistics for attack strength, defense strength, and movement points. These statistics are listed in a shorthand, code-like set of numbers called the ADM, which stands for Attack/Defense/Movement. You can find each unit's ADM numbers in the Civilopedia. In addition, military units have hit points. The vertical *health bar* (to the left of the unit) indicates how many hit points that unit potentially has and how many it currently has. The bar's color warns you of the unit's general condition.

*Attack strength shows the likelihood of inflicting damage when attacking an opponent.* Units with high attack strengths are useful for offensives (attacking the other unit first).

*Defense strength represents the ability of a unit to defend itself when attacked; it is the likelihood that damage will be inflicted on an attacking unit.* Units with high defense strengths are useful for defending cities and other positions against enemy troops. The terrain on which a unit stands can also increase its defensive strength.

*Movement points indicate how far a unit can travel in a turn;* they're explained in detail in **Chapter 7: Terrain and Movement**, too.

*Hit points indicate how much damage a unit can withstand before it is destroyed.* Units with a greater number of hit points can absorb more damage in combat. A green health bar indicates that a unit has most of its hit points remaining, a yellow health bar means the unit has been seriously damaged, and a red health bar shows that a unit is dangerously near destruction. Hit points can be restored by skipping turns (pressing the Spacebar), especially in cities with repair facilities. There is one exception to this rule: units do not recuperate when they're within enemy borders. A unit can gain additional hit points by earning veteran and later elite rank.

Units can be on *active* status, which means they are activated (take their turn as the "active unit") each turn. *Fortified* or *garrisoned* units are inactive, and they remain so even if rival units approach them, though they will defend themselves if attacked. A unit carrying out any order that takes more than one turn is *busy*. Clicking on a fortified, garrisoned, or busy unit activates that unit, and when the unit is active, you can give it new orders.

Units can "see" only into adjacent terrain squares, unless they are on high terrain (such as hills or mountains) or looking across water. In those cases, it can see twice as far—but even a unit on a mountain can't see over an adjacent mountain.

Early in the game, when most of the map is black, the observation limits are obvious. Every square is either *seen*, *explored*, or *dark*. Dark areas are veiled in darkness and completely unexplored. Explored areas that are not currently seen (by you) are dimmed. Seen squares are bright.

As time passes and you develop refinements and new advances, you can replace old units with a progression of ever more capable ones. Modern units often fulfill specialized roles, and some have unique capabilities. You can also *upgrade* your older units in any city that has a Barracks improvement *and* is able to build the new unit. Move the unit into the city and press [U].

For a chart of all the unit numbers and attributes, see the **Appendix**.

# Military Units

Through the years, much of your time is spent moving and positioning your "defense" forces. A strong military is, after all, the best defense against rivals and barbarians. Military units are also your eyes, exploring and monitoring the world as they move. Finally, they serve your offensive needs by defeating rival units and capturing enemy cities.

Your military forces can be ground units (Legions, Cannons, and Horsemen, for example), naval units (Galleys, Ironclads, Battleships, etc.), or air units (Fighters, Bombers, and Helicopters). Non-military units are discussed in detail a little later. All units, whether they are combat or non-combat oriented, are described in the Civilopedia.

## Ground Units

The majority of the units in the game are ground units. These forces move over the map square by square. They spend movement points according to the type of terrain they are entering, and they attack rival units when you move them into a square containing an enemy unit. Most ground units have an observation range of one square, unless they're standing on a Hill or Mountain square.

Ground units can also *pillage*—that is, strip the countryside they're crossing of any improvements Worker units have built, tearing up roads, filling in irrigation ditches, and collapsing mines.

## Naval Units

Naval units move only through water squares and cities. Some naval units (Galleys, Caravels, Galleons, and Transports) can carry ground units as passengers. Carriers can transport air units, and Submarines can transport missile units.

Many naval units can conduct bombardment—that is, they can bombard units or cities on land squares. This type of bombardment works in much the same way as the Bombard ability of ground units. Nuclear Submarines can carry Tactical Nukes. No other subs can carry any other kind of missile. Submarines can travel underwater, which hides them from most units' view, but some units (Aegis Cruisers, for example) can spot submarines if they are up to two squares away.

## Air Units

You do not move air units like you do other units. Instead, you assign them to missions. All air units must be based in a friendly city or on a Carrier.

When an air unit is the active unit, you'll notice some new Orders buttons. Use these to assign a mission to the unit. The possibilities are:

- **Bombing Mission:** Bombard on the selected terrain square or enemy city. Air bombardment affects units, city improvements, and city populations.

- **Recon Mission:** Investigate the selected square.

- **Re-base Mission:** Relocate the unit's base of operations to another city or an aircraft Carrier.

- **Air Superiority Mission:** Attack any and all enemy air units found within the unit's defensive range (half of its operational range). This is similar to the Fortify order in that it remains the unit's assignment until you reactivate the unit in order to give it other orders. Only fighters (including the F-15) are capable of flying air superiority missions.

- **Airdrop Mission:** Carry a single ground unit to a specified location, land, and drop the unit off, leaving it there. Only Helicopters can airdrop ground units, and then only within their operational range. This "vertical insertion" cannot place a unit into a square that contains an enemy unit.

Certain air units can carry out these missions, but only if a suitable target is within its *operational range.* The range is outlined on the map in the same way as the range for bombardment, and the same cross-hairs help you to find appropriate targets. Air units can cross any type of terrain to fulfill their mission, but they don't spend movement points according to the terrain, nor do they get any bonus for crossing squares improved by roads or railroads. Assigned missions take one turn to complete.

### Missiles

If a city is the target of a normal cruise missile attack, the city suffers a bombard attack. A nuclear missile attack destroys half the population, regardless of nationality. Military units have a 50% chance of surviving a nuclear attack. In addition to the loss of units, cities, and improvements, all land terrain squares adjacent to the impact square become polluted.

As you might expect, all missile units are one-shot attackers. They're always destroyed as part of the process of attacking. Note that missiles are considered air units and function identically to planes with regard to movement.

## Leaders and Armies

When an elite unit wins a battle, there is a chance that a great leader will emerge. A leader can achieve great deeds, like finishing a city's building project or building an army.

**Finish a great work:** When it arrives at a city that's in the midst of building a unit, a Wonder, or a city improvement, a leader can whip the population into a productivity frenzy, so that they finish the project in one turn.

**Create an Army:** A leader in a city can build an army there. An army is a ground unit that can contain other ground units (much like a seagoing transport unit carries units). Armies have a significant offensive advantage; when units are grouped together in an army, they attack as a team. For example, if your army consisted of several Archers, each Archer would attack and fight until it was reduced to one hit point. Then, the next Archer would take over. The battle would continue in this way until the enemy was defeated or you reached your last Archer (who would fight to the end as in any other combat).

Note that, whichever option you choose, the leader is used up in the process.

## Combat

Combat occurs when a unit enters a map square occupied by a rival unit or city. Battles are resolved immediately. If the unit under attack has no ability to defend itself (Workers, Settlers, Scouts, and similar units), it is captured without a fight.

Most battles result in the destruction of a unit (see "Retreat" below for the exceptions). When more than one unit occupies the defender's square, the unit with the highest defensive strength defends. If the attacker defeats the only unit in a square, it occupies

the now vacant square after the fight. If there are multiple units in the square, however, the attacker returns to its original square.

## A Note on Capturing Units

You can capture artillery units (Catapult, Cannons, and such), but only if you already have the advance that would allow you to build the unit. That is, if your civilization doesn't yet understand how a unit works, you can't capture it and use it.

## Retreat

"He who fights and runs away lives to fight another day." Few units in the game adhere to that maxim, but those that do can be very useful to a resourceful ruler. When a fast ground unit (the Horseman is a good example) attacks or is attacked, it fights until it has one remaining hit point, then moves away from the battlefield. Of course, if the unit is surrounded by inaccessible squares (oceans and enemies), it has nowhere to run and cannot retreat. When the battle involves an equally nimble opponent (such as another Horseman), retreat is not possible.

## Hit Points and Damage

Hit points are graphically indicated by the colored health bar near each unit. Both the length of the health bar (the number of segments) and the color are significant. As a unit loses hit points in an attack, its health bar gets shorter. In addition, when the unit is reduced to approximately two-thirds of its full strength, the health bar changes from green to yellow. When a unit's hit points are reduced to around one-third of its full strength, the bar changes from yellow to red.

Hit points represent a unit's relative durability in combat situations. Newly built units generally have 3 hit points. Veteran units have 4, and elite units have 5. A unit with 3 hit points can take three points of damage before being destroyed.

Successful attackers that have movement points remaining after combat can continue moving normally—and some can even attack again. However, successful attackers often sustain damage in each battle, and resting between fights is recommended.

**In Trouble**

**Different-colored health bars indicate levels of hurt.**

**Injured**            **Healthy**

## Healing

A damaged unit can take time to heal by skipping its entire turn (press the Spacebar). Units heal faster when they remain in cities for a full turn. If the city they occupy has certain improvements, they can heal even more rapidly. Along with its capacity for turning out veteran units, a Barracks can repair ground units. A Harbor can repair naval units. Airports and Carriers repair air units. In all these cases, the damaged unit is restored to full strength in a single turn.

Note that units do not regenerate as long as they are within the cultural border of a foreign civilization (with one exception; see **Chapter 10: Wonders**). Neither do air units based on Carriers.

## Terrain Modifiers

The terrain the defending unit occupies makes a difference in combat. Each type of terrain has a "defense value" that it lends to any unit defending itself in that terrain. This

can greatly increase a unit's chance of surviving an attack. For example, while a unit standing on plains (defense value of 10) doesn't get much tactical help from the flat landscape, the same unit hiding in the rugged mountains (defense value of 100) would enjoy a much greater chance of victory. The defense values of all the terrain types are listed in the **Appendix**.

## Calculating the Winner

Combat is essentially like a rapid-fire boxing match. Units fight one-on-one rounds, with damage being subtracted from the hit points of the loser of each round. When one unit loses all its hit points, it is destroyed.

The important factors in combat are the attack and defense strengths of the combatants, as well as their hit points, the presence of veteran or elite units on either side, the terrain occupied by the defender, and any defensive improvements in the square. In addition to considering all of these factors, combat also includes an element of chance. Sometimes a unit just gets lucky. We don't want to drag you through lots of heavy arithmetic for each combination of factors, but the calculations for each round of combat can be boiled down to a simple comparison.

The total modified attack and defense factors are combined, and the probability of either side winning is approximately the ratio of each side's factor compared to this total. For example, if a Knight (attack factor 4) attacks a Spearman (defense factor 2), the total of the factors is 6 (4 + 2). The Knight has about a 66% chance (4 out of 6) of winning each round.

The battle rages until one or the other completely loses its health bar. It is possible for one opponent to win every round and take no damage at all, and it is possible for the opponents to trade damage for damage until even the eventual winner is badly beaten up. Most battles fall somewhere in the middle.

## Adding in Adjustments

How do the adjustments for terrain and so on work? They're added into each factor they affect before the total is determined. For instance, if the Spearman is behind city Walls (which adds 50% to a unit's defense factor, making the Spearman a 3), the odds are changed to 4 out of 7 for the Knight and only 3 out of 7 for the Spearman.

# Special Combat Cases

To better reflect their real-world abilities and handicaps, some units have unique combat rules and abilities. There are a number of special combat situations, which have special rules, detailed below.

## Air Battles

Only units capable of flying air superiority missions (like Fighters) can attack other air units. When an enemy air unit flies into the defensive radius of an air unit flying air superiority, the defending units have a chance of shooting down the incoming enemy with no damage to the city. Of course, the enemy might also get through and complete its mission. Note that defending air units gain no combat benefits from city improvements—even SAM Missile Batteries.

## Bombardment

Artillery units (Catapults, Cannons, and all Artillery units) and warships (Frigate, Man-o-War, Ironclad, Destroyer, Battleship, Aegis Cruiser) have the ability to *bombard* a target that's within their range. Bombardment is an attack that does not involve moving into the same square as the defender. It's a "stand-off" or "ranged" attack. The attacker takes no risk of damage.

Bombardment affects everything in the target square, not just enemy units. The projectiles you launch might damage defensive fortifications like Fortresses and city Walls, harm military units, destroy a portion of a city's population, or demolish city improvements.

Note that the bombing attacks of fighters and bombers work in much the same way as this type of bombardment.

## City Defenses

Just by standing inside a city or metropolis, a unit gains a defensive bonus. The larger a settlement's population, the better the innate defense it provides to military units stationed or garrisoned there.

The Walls improvement raises the defense strength of units within a town (size 6 or less) by 50%—the same bonus given by a city (size 7–12). This boost is applicable to attacks by all ground units. (Note that units inside a city of size 7 or more get no bonus from Walls.) The Coastal Fortress increases the defense strength of all units within a city by 50% against naval attacks. The Coastal Fortress can also take shots at passing enemy ships.

## Fortresses

Units within a Fortress gain significant advantages. A unit stationed within a Fortress has its defensive strength increased by 50%, and it gains the ability to take "free shots" at passing enemy units. Once your civilization has discovered Construction, Worker units can build Fortresses on any terrain square (except a city square).

## Naval Blockades

You can blockade a rival civilization if you are at war with them. Just position your ships in every sea square surrounding an enemy Harbor, and no trade can get through. Likewise, your ships can be positioned at a naval chokepoint to have a similar effect.

## Nuclear Attacks

You launch a nuclear attack in the same way you target an air unit bombing mission. All units in the target square and adjacent squares have only a 50% chance of surviving, regardless of their cultural allegiance (in other words, both theirs and yours). In addition, a bombed city loses half its population. The defense against most nuclear attacks is the Small Wonder SDI Defense.

# Settlers and Workers

Settlers are groups of your most resourceful and adventurous citizens. As independent pioneers, they perform a critical function for your civilization: they found new cities. No other unit has this vital ability.

Workers serve as civil engineers, improving the terrain for your empire's benefit. At first, their skills are fairly limited, but as your civilization discovers advances, they develop more talents and better equipment.

Your civilization produces Settlers and Workers in the same manner as it does any other unit, with one caveat. When one of these units is completed, the population of the city

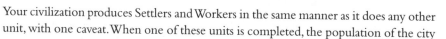

that produced it is reduced by one for Workers and by *two* for Settlers, representing the emigration of these pioneers.

## Founding and Adding to Cities

To found a new city, move a Settler to the desired location and click the Build order or press [B]. The unit disappears, as the people it represents become the first population point of the new city.

The same order can be used to increase the size of an existing city. Move a Settler or a Worker into an existing city and click the Join City order (or press [B]). The unit is absorbed into the city. A Worker adds one point to the population; a Settler adds two.

## Making Improvements

Workers can make a number of agricultural and industrial improvements to your civilization's topography. Each task takes a number of turns to complete, depending on the terrain being improved. Some improvements can only be undertaken after your civilization has acquired certain technologies. Workers are also the only units that can improve terrain.

Teamwork makes these units work faster. You can combine Workers to accomplish tasks more rapidly. For example, two Workers work twice as rapidly as one, and three can accomplish a task in one-third the standard time.

There is no limit to the number of times your Workers can build new improvements on any given terrain square. If the changing needs of your civilization demand clearing, irrigation, reforestation, clearing, pollution cleanup (detoxification), and reforestation in succession, the land can take it. If the order button you want doesn't appear in the usual place, it's because the task cannot be accomplished on that square at this time. Perhaps undertaking another improvement will make the desired option available in the future. For instance, a Jungle square cannot be irrigated. You'll need to convert it to a Plains square first, then you can irrigate.

We've included all of the variations in a table that lists the task, the shortcut key, the required advance (if any), and the terrain types that benefit from this improvement. Full explanations of each activity appear after the table.

| Order | Task | Shortcut Key | Required Advance | Terrains That Benefit |
|---|---|---|---|---|
| | Irrigate (fresh water) | I | — | Desert, Grassland, Plains, Flood Plains |
| | Irrigate (without water) | I | Electricity | Desert, Grassland, Plains, Flood Plains |
| | Clear | Shift-C | — | Forest |
| | | Shift-C | — | Jungle |
| | Build Fortress | Ctrl-F | Construction | Any Land Square |
| | Mine | M | — | Desert, Hills, Mountains, Plains, Grassland |
| | Reforest | N | Engineering | Grassland, Plains, Tundra |
| | Clean Up Pollution | Shift-C | — | Any Polluted Land Square |
| | Build Road | R | — | Any Land Square |
| | Build Railroad | Shift-R | Steam Power | Any Road Square |
| | Build Colony | B | — | Any Land Square |
| | Irrigate to City | Ctrl-I | — | (Automated) |
| | Road To | Ctrl-R | — | Any Land Square |
| | Railroad To | Ctrl-Shift-R | Steam Power | Any Land Square |
| | Road then Colony | Ctrl-B | — | Any Land Square |
| | Trade Network | Ctrl-N | — | (Automated) |

## Irrigate

Irrigation can improve the agricultural production of a city's terrain. (The form of government you rule under can limit the improvement. See "Governments" in **Chapter 12: Managing Your Empire** for details.) A suitable square can always be irrigated if it shares a side or a diagonal with a source of fresh water (terrain with a river running through it, a freshwater lake, or another irrigated square). Sometimes you might find it necessary to irrigate squares to which your city has no access in order to extend irrigation into squares the city uses. After you've discovered Electricity, your Workers can irrigate squares without fresh water. When your Worker is in the appropriate square, click the Irrigate order or press [I].

To have the Worker irrigate the square they're in, then irrigate every square in a continuous path linking the Worker's current location to the nearest city, press [Ctrl]-[I].

## Clear

Clearing terrain is a low-tech, labor-intensive form of land transformation, available only for some terrain types. Clearing improves the movement point cost of dense terrain (although it also eliminates the defensive bonus) and provides land suitable to further improvement through irrigation and such. Sometimes, a terrain square might need to be cleared to allow for irrigation, then later reforested to restore valuable resources. When your Worker is in the appropriate square, click the Clear order or press [Shift]-[C].

## Build Fortress

Building Fortresses can be essential for defense of terrain that is not a city site. Fortresses provide a defensive bonus to rural or frontier units in the same way the Walls improvement benefits urban defensive units (see "Combat" for the full details). When your Worker is in the appropriate square, click the Build Fortress order or press [Ctrl]-[F].

## Mine

Mining terrain allows full exploitation of the natural resources present—it increases the number of shields you collect from the square. When your Worker is in the appropriate square, click the Build Mine order or press [M].

## Reforest

Click this order to reforest a square that's devoid of trees. This results in a change in the square's terrain type, generally for the better. When your Worker is in the appropriate square, click the Reforest order or press [N].

## Clean Up Pollution

Detoxifying a square by cleaning up the pollution there restores the full (pre-pollution) production capacity of the affected square. Both industrial pollution and nuclear contamination can be eliminated by cleanup efforts. When your Worker is in the appropriate square, click the Clean Up Pollution order or press [Shift]-[C].

## Build Road

Building roads across terrain reduces the movement point cost of that square to one-third of a point, provided that the moving unit enters from an adjacent road square. It also improves the commerce production of the square. When your Worker is in the appropriate square, click the Build Road order or press [R].

To build a continuous road linking the Worker's current location to another square, press [Ctrl]-[R]. You'll need to select the destination square, in the same way as you do for a GoTo order.

You can also assign your Worker to a long-term project: building an unbroken network of roads linking all of your cities and all of the special natural resources within your borders. To start this ambitious undertaking, press [Ctrl]-[N].

## Build Railroads

Laying track across terrain eliminates the movement point cost of that square, providing the moving unit enters from an adjacent railroad square. Railroads also increase the yields of both irrigation and mines. You can only build them where you have already built roads. In addition, railroads require both Iron and Coal. When your Worker is in the appropriate square, click the Build Railroads order or press [Shift]-[R].

To build a continuous railroad linking the Worker's current location to another square, use [Ctrl]-[Shift]-[R]. You'll need to select the destination square, in the same way as you do for a GoTo order.

### Build Colony

Sometimes you find out too late—after you've built a city—that there's a great strategic resource or luxury just a few squares outside the City Radius. You can't wait until the city's border expands to bring it under your dominion; you need the resource *now*. If you have a Worker available, you can solve this problem by building a *colony*.

A colony is not a city, but rather a small settlement with a specific purpose. It gives any city that's connected to it access to the strategic resource or luxury in the colonized square. When your Worker is in the appropriate square, click the Build Colony order or press [B].

To first build a road linking the square the Worker's currently in to the prospective colony site, *then* establish the colony, use [Ctrl]-[B]. You'll need to select the destination square, in the same way as you do for a GoTo order.

---

### Automated Workers

If you tire of giving orders to your Workers, you can turn control over to a subordinate. Use the Automate Worker order (or press [A]) to put the unit "on automatic" for a while. Automated units improve the terrain around your cities, and they'll also establish roads between cities. If you want to limit the automated Worker's efforts to only the city it's currently nearest, use [Shift]-[I] instead. If you press [Shift]-[A], the automated Worker will not replace already existing improvements. For example, if you use [Shift]-[A], the automated Worker will not mine an irrigated Desert.

---

## Explorers

Explorers are non-combat units that treat all terrain as if there were roads across it. That is, movement from square to square costs them only one-third of a point. Their bravery and resourcefulness makes them ideal for opening up new continents and discovering the far reaches of a landmass quickly. The risk is that Explorers, like Settlers and Workers, have no way to defend themselves and can be captured by any military unit.

# Barbarians

Barbarians are small tribes of raiders that are not part of any opposing civilization. They always carry the color white. You can set the likelihood and frequency of barbarian attacks in the initial game choices you make. You will encounter them periodically as your civilization begins to expand and grow. They arise from villages in unsettled parts of any continent. Barbarians will attack your units and plunder your cities.

Because barbarians can appear in any unsettled area, it is important to defend your cities with at least one military unit. Barbarians (and rival units) can walk right into an undefended city.

Barbarians arise in areas that are outside the borders of any civilization. They will appear at the same distance from civilizations. Thus, expanding your network of cities over a continent eventually removes the threat of barbarians, because the entire area has become more or less civilized by your urban presence.

When you find and invade a barbarian tribe's encampment, you wipe out the threat that particular group posed. The village is destroyed and will create no more units. (Any units already outside the village, however, continue to exist.) You also gain financially, as some of the horde's plunder is always found in the village.

# CIVILIZATION ADVANCES

*"It is in the pursuit and study of the natural sciences that mankind provides the greatest evidence of his nobility, of his spark of the divine."*

As humankind progressed by fits and starts through the ages, civilizations rose and fell, their success or failure due to what knowledge they acquired and how they employed it.

Those who first acquire new knowledge are often able to employ it to build a more powerful position, but there have been many cases when civilizations obtained some new invention first and failed to use it to their advantage. The pace at which a society develops and implements new knowledge depends on many factors, including its social organization, economic organization, geographic location, leadership, and competition.

**Science Advisor**

Great One, our Prophets have learned the secret of Bronze Working. What shall we explore now?

The Wheel (20 turns)

OK. Sounds good.

What's the big picture?

The concept that progress is inevitable—or even that it's desirable—is a relatively recent phenomenon. For most of human history, the pace of progress was so slow as to be barely detectable, but since the Industrial Revolution, the pace of advance and change has dramatically increased. Rapid change is now considered normal.

## The Concept of Civilization Advances

Scientific research is what drives your civilization's intellectual growth. The science each city generates every turn represents spending on research, a percentage of the total income from commerce the city brings in. You can adjust this percentage (for your civilization as a whole) with the Science Rate controller on the Domestic Advisor's screen. A low science rate generates advances slowly; a high rate generates them more quickly.

You want to accumulate research to gain *civilization advances*. The scientific research being performed by each city in your empire is listed in the Domestic Advisor's report. Each new advance that your civilization discovers "costs" a certain amount of science. As you progress, more advanced technologies require more funding to research. The Science Advisor notes the advances you already have, the one your scientists are currently researching, and any plans for future research you've specified. Almost all new *advances allow your civilization to build new units, city improvements, or Great Wonders.*

Most new civilization advances also open up a path to researching further discoveries. You can think of the connections between advances as a flowchart, a web, a tree, or whatever image works for you. The important idea is that *each advance is a building block that allows research into further advances.* You can even eventually research into the realm of science fiction; each futuristic advance you discover adds bonus points to your final score, as we'll explain below in "Future Technology."

Accumulated research isn't the only way to gain advances. Contact with a minor tribe might also net you a new civilization advance. Finally, during parley with other civilizations, you can sometimes get or give advances in trade. We'll give you the full details under **Chapter 13: Diplomacy and Trade.**

Civilization advances are organized into *ages.* Your civilization must successfully gain all of the critical technologies of an age before moving on to research advances that belong to the next age. Of course, learning *all* the advances in an age is your best bet.

# Climbing the Technology Tree

Once your civilization begins to accumulate scientific research, your Science Advisor asks you to choose a new civilization advance to research. He suggests a line to pursue, but before you just accept his choice, take a look at the options. Click the arrow to the right of his suggestion to choose from a drop-down list of the advances you could research right now. If what you want is on the list, great. If not, use the Big Picture option to open the Science Advisor's screen.

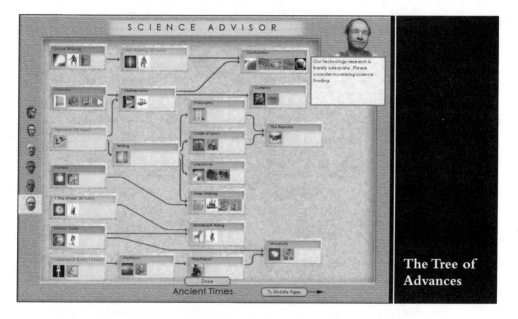

The Tree of Advances

The Science Advisor presents all the possible avenues of research in the form of a handy flowchart. This chart not only shows the research that's available to you now, it charts the entire future of science. You can use the arrows near the bottom of the screen to move between the ages of scientific discovery. You can take a look at the Civilopedia entry for any advance by right-clicking on the name of the advance. The entries for any units, improvements, or Wonders are also just a click away.

When you decide which advance you're most interested in pursuing, just click on it. All the advances you need to research in order to reach your goal are selected for you and queued up. Unless you give them other instructions, your scientists will follow this line of research until you reach your goal.

If you know the next few advances you wish to research, but they don't lie directly along the line to some future goal, that's okay. You can establish your own research queue, advance by advance. After you have selected the first advance (#1), hold down the [Shift] key and select another advance. Voilà! In this way, you can line up several advances, and you won't have to worry that your scientists will get off track while you're preoccupied with other matters. (They'll still check with you between projects, just in case you change your mind.)

Once you have chosen your next research project, your scientists pursue that topic until they learn the new civilization advance—or until you change their focus. That's right, you can interrupt research in progress. If you go to the Science Advisor's screen, then click on the new advance you want your researchers to work on, they'll put their efforts there. Of course, by changing their focus, you lose all of their work on the advance you order them to abandon.

When research is complete, your chief investigator announces the discovery. If the new advance gives you the ability to use a previously unrecognized strategic resource, sources of it become visible on your World Map. The production menus in each City Display are immediately revised to include any new items the advance makes possible— wherever they are appropriate. How could an item be inappropriate? One example is that inland cities can never build ships, so ship units never appear on their production menus, even if you have discovered seafaring advances. Another is that cities without access to the requisite strategic resources (Horses for mounted units, for instance) cannot build certain items.

After you acquire a new advance, your Science Advisor appears again to ask for a new topic to research (or to verify your previous instructions). The list of choices is updated with each new discovery to reflect your growing knowledge base. Advances you acquire from minor tribes and diplomacy no longer appear on the list of choices since you've already discovered them. If by chance you're given the civilization advance your scientists are currently researching, your Science Advisor immediately switches the research effort to a new topic of your choice.

## Optional Advances

To move forward from one scientific age to the next (and gain access to the advances in that age), you're required to successfully research *almost* all of the advances available in your current age. The only exceptions are advances that fall into the category of optional.

## Ancient

- Horseback Riding
- Literature
- Monarchy
- Republic

## Middle Ages

- Chivalry
- Democracy
- Economics
- Free Artistry
- Military Tradition
- Music Theory
- Navigation
- Printing Press

## Industrial

- Advanced Flight
- Amphibious Warfare
- Communism
- Espionage
- Nationalism
- Sanitation

These advances are not required, but can certainly be useful. Optional advances frequently make construction of Great Wonders possible.

# Future Technology

After your scientists discover the last of the named advances, they can begin researching futuristic advances. These not-yet-imagined civilization advances are collectively known as "Future Technology." When your civilization accumulates enough scientific research to finish one unit of Future Technology, you can research another. Each Future Technology you discover adds to your final score (see "Scoring" in **Chapter 14: Winning the Game** for other ways to boost your final total).

# Special Advance Effects

A number of the advances have effects independent of the new units and improvements you can build. We summarize these effects here. Each advance's Civilopedia entry also lists all of its effects.

### Ancient Advances

**Construction:** Workers can build Fortresses.

**Iron Working:** The strategic resource Iron appears on the World Map.

**Mapmaking:** You gain the ability to trade maps.

**The Wheel:** The strategic resource Horses appears on the World Map.

**Writing:** Allows you to establish Embassies, sign right of passage agreements and military alliances, and trade communications with other civilizations.

### Middle Ages Advances

**Astronomy:** Allows trade to take place over Sea squares.

**Engineering:** Workers can plant forests. Knowledge of bridge building causes movement bonuses to apply when crossing a river on a road.

**Gunpowder:** The strategic resource Saltpeter appears on the World Map.

**Magnetism:** Allows trade over Ocean squares.

**Navigation:** Allows trade over Ocean squares.

## Industrial Advances

**Electricity:** Workers can irrigate from any source of water.

**Nationalism:** Allows you to sign mutual protection pacts and trade embargoes. Nationalism also allows you to *mobilize* your economy. This allows you to draft citizens to create military units.

**Refining:** The strategic resource Oil appears on the World Map.

**Replaceable Parts:** The strategic resource Rubber appears on the World Map. Doubles the work rate of Workers.

**Steam Power:** Workers can upgrade roads to railroads. The strategic resource Coal appears on the World Map.

## Modern Advances

**Fission:** The strategic resource Uranium appears on the World Map.

**Rocketry:** The strategic resource Aluminum appears on the World Map.

# 10 WONDERS

*"The measure of a great ruler is the monuments she leaves behind."*

A Wonder of the World—whether it's a Great Wonder or a Small Wonder—is a dramatic, awe-inspiring accomplishment. It is typically a great achievement of engineering, science, or the arts, representing a milestone in history. As your civilization progresses through the years, certain advances make building Wonders of the World possible. These and the Small Wonders are the extraordinary monuments of a civilization, bringing everlasting glory and other benefits to their owners.

## The Concept of Wonders

Both types of Wonders are like extraordinary city improvements, in that they are structures (or achievements) that you can undertake. Unlike city improvements, *each Great Wonder is unique*, existing only in the city where it is constructed. Small Wonders are not unique, but each civilization can build only one of each.

Small Wonders are Wonders that either are not quite remarkable enough to be unique or have such useful benefits that it's not fair (that is, it makes the game less fun) to limit them to one civilization. Great Wonders have prerequisite civilization advances, similar to city improvements. In contrast, Small Wonders are made possible by a civilization making specific achievements. Every civilization can build the same Small Wonders, but only after they have accomplished the prerequisite achievement.

Every Wonder confers a specific benefit on the civilization that owns it (you can find the specifics in the Civilopedia listing for each Wonder). If a Great Wonder is captured (along with the city it's in), its benefits go to the new owner. Small Wonders in a city are always destroyed when the city is captured.

*If a Wonder of the World is destroyed by the decimation of the city in which it stood, it can never be rebuilt.* Its benefits are lost to the world forever. Further, some of the glories of certain Wonders dim over time. Objects and accomplishments that awed the ancients lose their luster for people of the modern age. *The achievement of later advances can negate the benefits of older Wonders.* The cultural benefits of a Wonder continue to accrue unless the Wonder is destroyed.

# Building Wonders

You can build a Great Wonder only if you have discovered the advance that makes it possible—and if it doesn't already exist somewhere else in the world. Wonders can be built in any city, and you can build more than one in the same city.

If you are building a Great Wonder in one of your cities and the same Wonder is completed elsewhere before you finish, you must convert your production to something else. Any excess shields are lost, so be careful what you choose.

Wonders are often long-term projects, as befits their magnificence. If you want to complete construction of a Wonder faster than the city that is building it can generate shields, you have only one option: use a leader. There is no other method of hurrying a Wonder project.

## Destroying Wonders

Great Wonders are not destroyed when an enemy captures the city in which they exist. However, if a city possessing one is razed, that Wonder is lost forever and cannot be rebuilt.

# The Benefits of Wonders

Each Wonder has both specific and general benefits. You can read about the specific benefits in the appropriate Civilopedia entry or in the charts that follow. The glory—and

culture points—that accrue to your civilization for possessing a Wonder are the general benefits conferred by such great works; more importantly, these benefits continue to accrue even if new advances make the Wonder's specific benefit obsolete.

| Small Wonder | Effect(s) |
| --- | --- |
| *Ancient* | |
| Forbidden Palace | Lowers corruption as if it were a second capital |
| Heroic Epic | Increases the likelihood of leaders appearing |
| Iron Works | Production increased by 100% in the city |
| *Medieval* | |
| Military Academy | Can build Armies in the city without a leader |
| Wall Street | Treasury earns interest every turn |
| *Industrial* | |
| Battlefield Medicine | Allows military units to heal in enemy territory |
| Intelligence Agency | Enables you to undertake Espionage missions |
| The Pentagon | All Armies' troop capacity increased |
| *Modern* | |
| Apollo Program | Allows construction of spaceship parts |
| Strategic Missile Defense | Chance of intercepting ICBM attacks |

| Great Wonder | Effect(s) |
| --- | --- |
| *Ancient* | |
| The Colossus | Adds one Commerce to all squares where you're producing Commerce |
| The Great Library | Gives you any advance already known by two other known civilizations |
| The Great Lighthouse | Galleys travel safely in Sea squares<br>Movement allowance of all naval units increased by 1 |
| The Great Wall | Doubles the defense bonus for all your Walls<br>Your units' combat values are doubled versus barbarians |
| The Hanging Gardens | Makes 3 content citizens happy in the city where it's built and 1 in all others |
| The Oracle | Doubles the happiness effect of all Temples in your cities |
| The Pyramids | Puts a Granary in all your cities on the same continent |

| Great Wonder | Effect(s) |
|---|---|
| **Medieval** | |
| Adam Smith's Trading Company | Pays maintenance for all trade-related city improvements |
| Copernicus' Observatory | Doubles research in the city where it's built |
| JS Bach's Cathedral | Makes 2 unhappy citizens content in all your cities on the same continent |
| Leonardo's Workshop | Reduces the cost of upgrading units by 50% |
| Magellan's Great Voyage | All your naval units gain 1 extra movement point |
| Michelangelo's Chapel | Doubles the happiness effect of all Cathedrals |
| Newton's University | Scientific research in the city that builds it is doubled |
| Shakespeare's Theater | 8 unhappy citizens are made content |
| Sun Tzu's Art of War | Provides the benefits of a Barracks in all your cities |
| **Industrial** | |
| Hoover Dam | Provides the benefits of a Hydro Plant to all your cities on the same continent |
| The United Nations | Makes Diplomatic Victory possible |
| Theory of Evolution | Gain two free civilization advances |
| Universal Suffrage | Reduces war weariness in all your cities |
| **Modern** | |
| Cure for Cancer | Makes 1 unhappy citizen content in each of your cities |
| Longevity | Cities grow by 2 citizens (instead of 1) when the Food Storage Box fills |
| SETI Program | Doubles science research in its city |
| The Manhattan Project | Allows all civilizations to build nuclear weapons |

# MANAGING YOUR CITIES

*"Cities are like lovers. Treat them well—but not too well—and you will get what you want from them."*

Each city has different assets and demands, so each should be managed somewhat differently from the others. You should keep several goals in mind when managing a city: maintaining population growth, maximizing a useful mix of economic development (food and materials), producing commercial income for research and your treasury, and building useful units and improvements—all the while maintaining an attitude of contentment and thereby avoiding civil disorder. For cities to grow and prosper, they need to balance economic output with their citizens' needs for infrastructure and services.

## City Management Concepts

As your city increases in size, its population expands and it produces more and more bread (food), shields (production), and commerce. In city management, you add another layer of concepts that address how you turn these materials into products you can use. Refer to the City Display as you read.

Bread feeds your population. When a city produces more food than its population consumes each turn, the excess accumulates in the Food Storage Box. When the box is full, another citizen is added to the Population Roster and the city increases in size. If your city is not producing enough food each turn to feed its population, the shortfall is noted and stores are removed from the Food Storage Box. If the box empties, one citizen is removed from the Population Roster and your city decreases in size.

Experienced players should note that military units no longer require shield support from their city of origin. Support for military units comes out of your treasury. Settlers and Workers also do *not* require food support from their city of origin. They're supported with money from your treasury, like other units.

Shields power your industrial capacity. When a city produces shields, those shields accumulate in the Production Box. When the Production Box is full, your city produces something. It can "build" one of three kinds of things: units, which move around the map (like Settlers and Chariots); city improvements, which are tied to specific cities (like Libraries and Aqueducts); and Wonders of the World, which give great benefits to the civilization that builds them (like the Pyramids or Great Lighthouse). The type of government you choose and the distance remote cities are located from your palace affect your shield production. Production capacity is often lost to waste. You can read the details about waste under "Empire Management Concepts" in **Chapter 12: Managing Your Empire**.

Commerce provides the tax income you need to maintain your infrastructure, pay your armed forces, and engage in scientific research. Based on the tax rate you set, income from commerce is further divided. You control what portion of your tax income is spent on scientific research and entertainment. The rest is allocated to your treasury—after support costs (for units and city improvements) and any other expenses are deducted. Commerce income can also be lost to corruption. Your current type of government and the distance to your capital affect a city's level of corruption. You can read about corruption under "Empire Management Concepts" in **Chapter 12: Managing Your Empire**.

The Population Roster tells you more than just the number of citizens in your city. It also notes your citizens' nationality and their general level of contentment. Citizen icons appear in four different attitudes: *happy*, *content*, *unhappy*, and *resisting*. When you start building cities, you start with content citizens. As the population grows, some citizens become unhappy. You must balance unhappy citizens with happy citizens, or your city falls into *civil disorder*. Not only does civil disorder sound bad, it has all sorts of nasty consequences, as we'll explain shortly. Whenever you take over a city of another nationality (but not, usually, when you retake one of your own cities), some of the population there resist your rule. They stay that way until you make peace with their mother country or "win them over" and convince them to share in your culture—and go back to work. (They retain their nationality, however.)

For now, you need to know that you can increase the happiness of your citizens in several different ways: *building specific city improvements* like Temples and Cathedrals (see "City Improvements" below), *reassigning military units* (the explanation of military police appears under "Restoring Order" below), *making luxuries available to your cities*, and *increasing the amount of taxes spent on entertainment* (see "Population Roster" in **Chapter 15: Reference: Screen by Screen** for the details on this).

# Population Growth

Keeping a city's population growing is important because each additional citizen contributes something to your civilization. Each new citizen brings a new terrain square under production in your City Radius until there are no empty squares to work. After this point, each new citizen becomes a Specialist. Thus, population growth increases your economic power and, concurrently, the strength of your civilization. The size of your population is a major factor in determining your Civilization Score and is a measure of how well you have ruled.

- A *town* has a population of 6 or lower.

- It becomes a *city* when the population is 7–12.

- Above population 12, it's a *metropolis*.

# Resource Development

The citizens of a city who work the surrounding countryside harness the economic resources within the city's radius. Depending on the needs of your civilization, sometimes you may prefer increased industrial output from a particular city to other types. At other times, you'll want increased revenues. Still other times, sheer population growth might be the most important goal.

You can manipulate the output of a city by reassigning citizen laborers on the City Display. If you see city resource icons on a terrain square, that means a citizen is working there. Click on one of those squares to take the citizen off work and make an Entertainer out of him. Now click on an empty terrain square to put the Entertainer back to work. By experimenting with the placement of citizen laborers on the City Display, you can find the optimum production ratio of food to raw materials to commerce for that city.

Having an Entertainer on your Population Roster will change the attitude of one of your citizens. For more information on this reaction, see "Happiness and Civil Disorder" below.

## Tax Revenue

The percentage of your commerce income that is deposited into your treasury is determined by the research and entertainment rates you set on the Domestic Advisor's screen. Why do you need tax revenue anyway?

- You need cash to pay support for your units—those over and above your allotment of free units (based on your type of government, as discussed in "Governments" in **Chapter 12: Managing Your Empire**).

- Money is also useful because many of the improvements you build in your cities require a maintenance fee every turn.

- You can sometimes pay to speed up industrial production (see "Rush Jobs" below).

- You have to pay for espionage, especially propaganda campaigns to sway enemy cities over to your side (see "Espionage" in **Chapter 13: Diplomacy and Trade**).

- Last, but not least, cold currency is a medium of trade that can serve you well during negotiations with your neighbors (see "Conducting Diplomacy" in **Chapter 13: Diplomacy and Trade**).

The combined tax revenues of all your cities, after the research and entertainment percentages have been deducted, must exceed the combined maintenance and military support requirements before any can accumulate in your treasury. It is not necessary for every city to have a positive cash flow, but enough cities must be profitable to cover your civilization's expenses—or your treasury will be depleted to cover the deficit. You can watch the Treasury line in the Info Box or check with your Domestic Advisor to see if you have a surplus or a deficit.

Some cities might not be especially suited for industrial production because of terrain or other factors, but might still be good commerce centers and capable of generating lots of tax revenue. If you get to the point where you are no longer interested in building new items in a location, you can direct the city to build wealth by converting its shields into gold.

## Scientific Research

The greater the research contribution each city makes, the faster your people discover new civilization advances. The science rate you set determines the amount of research done in each city (see "Advisors" in **Chapter 15: Reference: Screen by Screen** for how to adjust the science rate).

You can influence a city's research contribution by adjusting the amount of commerce it generates (research is a fraction of commerce income), by creating Scientists, and by building certain city improvements. Improvements that can help are the Library, University, and Research Lab—plus some Wonders. **Chapter 9: Civilization Advances** goes into detail about how to read the advances tree.

## Entertainment

The greater the entertainment contribution each city makes, the happier your people are. The entertainment rate you set determines the amount of bonus happy faces created in each city (see "Advisors" in **Chapter 15: Reference: Screen by Screen** for how to adjust the science and entertainment rates).

## Industrial Production

Your most valuable cities can be those with the greatest industrial capacity, those cities whose citizens produce the greatest number of shields. These cities can quickly produce expensive military units with which you can extend the power of your civilization. They are also best at producing Wonders of the World, as Wonders generally cost immense numbers of shields. City management is a dynamic art; you must regularly monitor the production of your cities to ensure you are building the items you most need.

Several factors influence a city's production of shields. The terrain within your City Radius is most important, as citizens working on some types of terrain produce no shields at all (see **Chapter 7: Terrain and Movement** for further explanations). You might find it worthwhile to have Workers improve the terrain within your City Radius

to yield more or different resources. Beyond terrain, the form of government you choose for your civilization can affect the city's productivity (see "Governments" in the next chapter for these limitations).

There are a number of successful strategies for adjusting industrial capacity. The simplest is to shift citizens laboring on the City Display so that they produce more shields (see "Resource Development" earlier for instructions). You can also have Workers improve terrain within the City Radius to produce more shields. Within each city, you can order the construction of improvements such as a Factory, Hydro Plant (or other power plant), Manufacturing Plant, or Offshore Platform that increase shield production. Several Wonders also affect shield output. Consult the Civilopedia for the complete list of possible city improvements and Wonders. Each Civilopedia entry shows the construction and maintenance cost of each item, its purpose, and what advance is required to make it available.

### Note for Experienced Players

There is *no penalty* for switching production in midstream, unless the new project costs fewer shields than are already accumulated, in which case you forfeit the excess shields as overrun.

## City Governors

As you play, you'll undoubtedly notice that when a city completes a building project, it selects another one without your input. The city governors do this. Unless you give specific instructions, the governors will choose what to produce next by guessing at what you want. These guesses are based on the history of production orders you've given throughout the game.

The governors can be very useful, but only if they correctly interpret your previous orders. To help avoid problems, you can give your governors specific guidelines to follow in their selection of projects. At the City Display, press [G] to give instructions to that city's governors.

You can give instructions that cover only this city, all cities, or only those cities on the same continent as this one. On the General governor page, options are:

- **Manage citizens:** This gives the governors your permission to control the allocation of citizen laborers to the terrain in the City Radius. Using the next three options, you instruct them as to your priorities for this task. If you select more than one of these three, the governors strike a balance between those you've chosen.

  - **Emphasize food** – instructs the governors to maximize the food produced.

  - **Emphasize shields** – instructs the governors to maximize shield production.

  - **Emphasize commerce** – instructs the governors to maximize income from commerce.

- **Manage production:** This gives the governors your permission to assign building projects as they see fit. Using the next two options, you can put limits on what they're allowed to do.

  - **Never start Wonders** – tells the governors not to begin construction of a Wonder.

  - **Never start Small Wonders** – tells the governors not to begin construction of a Small Wonder.

Click the Production button to switch to the Production governor page. Here, you can give your governors some more detailed production orders. Specifically, for every one of the options, you can specify how often the governor should select to produce that particular thing. This effectively provides your governors with a list of priorities. You can set priorities for:

- **Offensive ground units** – those units that are stronger on offense than defense

- **Defensive ground units** – those units that are stronger on defense than offense

- **Artillery** – strictly offensive bombardment units, like Catapults

- **Settlers** – Settlers

- **Workers** – Workers

- **Naval units** – seagoing vessels

- **Air units** – flying units

- **Growth** – city improvements that increase the rate of population growth in the city

- **Production** – city improvements that improve the shield production in the city

- **Happiness** – city improvements that add to the happiness of your citizens

- **Science** – city improvements that boost the scientific research output of the city

- **Wealth** – city improvements that increase the tax income the city produces

- **Trade** – city improvements that augment the city's trading capacity and commerce

- **Exploration** – units whose primary role is exploration, like Scouts and Explorers

- **Culture** – city improvements that build the city's cultural influence

# City Protection

Great economic management of a city is worthless if the city is captured by rivals or plundered by barbarians. Therefore, part of your management plan must concern the defense of each city.

## Military Units

The minimum city defense is one combat unit, preferably one good at defending. A second defender can provide backup in case the first is taken out (see "Military Units" in **Chapter 8: Units** for the details of combat). A unit that's able to strike at enemies that move adjacent to the city is handy for weakening or perhaps destroying them before they launch an attack. Garrison any units that you expect to defend a city because garrisoned units gain defense strength—as explained more fully under "Military Units" in **Chapter 8: Units**.

## City Size and Walls

Defending units' defense abilities are modified by the size of the city they defend. The larger a city's population, the better the defense modifier. A town provides no defensive bonus, a city gives a 50% boost, and a metropolis provides a 100% bonus. In a town you can build Walls, which raise the defense to that of a size 7 city. (Walls have no effect in a city of size 7 or more.) Terrain bonuses are figured in before the city size and Walls take effect. Some units can destroy walls with their Bombard ability.

# City Improvements

City improvements represent the commercial, bureaucratic, educational, and public works infrastructure that make large and efficient cities possible. They also establish and build the cultural identity of the city. In the real world, New York City's dense population depends on the extensive subway system for transportation and buys electrical power generated by distant grids. Los Angeles is located in a desert and pipes in much of its water from sources hundreds of miles away. Paris is renowned worldwide for its museums and its history of patronage for the arts.

Improvements are critical to the growth and importance of cities. Inadequate provision of these facilities can limit the potential of a city. Each improvement provides some service or otherwise makes a city work more efficiently. You must choose which improvement to implement at what time. Does your city need a Marketplace or a Library more? Would a Courthouse provide more benefit than a Cathedral? Would a Temple speed up expansion of your borders? Some improvements specifically impact military units. For example, Barracks produce veteran ground units. Others improve your city's output, make the population happier, or aid in the city's defense.

A city's borders determine what nearby strategic resources and luxuries you can take advantage of. The expansion of these borders is, in turn, determined by the city's cultural development. You can only make real progress by building and maintaining those improvements that contribute to the city's cultural growth (such as Temples and Libraries).

Certain combinations of improvement dramatically increase production in a city, though there are some restrictions to this benefit. Discussing every city improvement in detail is beyond the scope of this manual, but all of the city improvements are listed in the Civilopedia. Each entry explains the building costs, benefits, and maintenance fees of each improvement, along with any conditions that might make the improvement obsolete or nonfunctional, so be sure to check them out.

# Losing Improvements

Improvements are not invulnerable, nor are they guaranteed to be permanent fixtures in an ever-dynamic city. They can be vulnerable to sabotage or bombardment. If you're really strapped for cash, you can even sell a city's improvements. All Small Wonders in a city are destroyed whenever it is captured. (Perhaps it goes without saying, but when a city is completely destroyed, all the improvements are destroyed with it.)

## Sabotage

The spies of a rival civilization can attempt to sabotage your city's infrastructure—and you can attempt to sabotage theirs. This might scrap the item that the city is currently producing or destroy half the shields committed to the current project. See **Chapter 13: Diplomacy and Trade** for the details on "diplomatic" actions. (There *are* defenses against this type of attack.)

# Selling Improvements

To raise cash, open the city's City Display and look at the Improvements Roster. Any improvement that is not a Wonder can be sold. Right-click on the name of an improvement you can do without to sell it. A dialog box shows how much you could get for selling the improvement and how much you could receive for selling that same improvement in all of your cities. To confirm the sale, click OK. If you sell, the improvement disappears from the city and the money is added to your treasury.

Selling improvements can be useful when you are short of money. It can also be useful when you are under attack with no reasonable chance of defending or recovering a city. By selling off its improvements, you reduce its value to the enemy and salvage something before you lose the city. You cannot sell Wonders of the World.

# Rush Jobs

Sometimes you need the benefits of an improvement right away, not 20 turns down the line. If your type of government allows it and you have sufficient funds, you can rush completion of an item by paying for it. Speeding construction in this manner, however, comes at a premium cost. When your citizens are rushed, they receive overtime wages and must pay surcharges on material delivery and fabrication. Rush jobs cost four times as much gold as the remaining shields needed for completion. (You cannot pay to rush a Wonder of the World.)

Under some forms of government, paying for a rush job isn't an option. You can, however, "spend" population points to hurry production. Your foremen use every means at their disposal to get more work out of your citizens for the same pay—including forcible coercion if necessary. As you might imagine, people don't enjoy working under those conditions, and they look for ways to leave town. By the time the work is done, emigration will have diminished the size of the city. (You can't spend population to rush a Wonder of the World.)

To rush a job without using either of these costly methods, you normally have two options. Any unit that you disband in a city contributes a portion of its cost in shields to the current construction project, whether it is an improvement or another unit. The other method is to clear forests in the city's radius. The resources gained from this action go straight into the construction project.

One way of completing a job in record time is available to you only if you have a leader and have not yet used it to create an Army. A leader, when entering a city, can complete whatever is under construction there. The leader disappears in the process, however, so this is not an action to be taken lightly. This is the only really effective way to rush the production of a Wonder of the World. Any leaders that you currently have available are listed on the Military Advisor's screen.

Items completed by rush jobs are available at the beginning of your next turn, so there is no advantage to rushing items that would be complete on the next turn anyway. To determine whether an item can be completed next turn without rushing, check the City Display. The number of turns to completion is noted in the Production Box and beneath the city on the Map screen.

# Culture

The definition of 'culture' is a slippery one. It can encompass anything that gives a civilization social cohesion, its members a sense of belonging to something greater than themselves. Culture contributes to feelings of nationality, pride of place, and the willingness to resist that which is alien. A strong culture can impress other nations.

Many things contribute to a city's cultural strength. Improvements, especially those generally considered enlightening, like a Library or a Temple, add to a city's culture. So do both kinds of Wonders. The longer a thing exists, the more venerable it becomes, and

thus it contributes more. Below are the numbers of points contributed by the various buildings each turn. During wartime footing, cultural improvements produce half the number normally produced per turn.

## City Improvements

| | |
|---|---|
| Cathedral | 3 |
| Colosseum | 2 |
| Library | 3 |
| Palace | 1 |
| Research Lab | 2 |
| Temple | 2 |
| University | 4 |

## Small Wonders

| | |
|---|---|
| Apollo Program | 3 |
| Battlefield Medicine | 1 |
| Forbidden Palace | 3 |
| Heroic Epic | 4 |
| Intelligence Agency | 1 |
| Iron Works | 2 |
| Military Academy | 1 |
| Strategic Missile Defense | 1 |
| The Pentagon | 1 |
| Wall Street | 2 |

## Wonders of the World

| | |
|---|---|
| Adam Smith's Trading Company | 3 |
| Copernicus' Observatory | 4 |
| Cure for Cancer | 5 |
| Hoover Dam | 3 |
| JS Bach's Grand Cathedral | 5 |
| Leonardo's Invention Workshop | 2 |
| Longevity | 3 |
| Magellan's Great Voyage | 3 |
| Michelangelo's Sistine Chapel | 4 |
| Newton's Great University | 5 |
| SETI Program | 3 |
| Shakespeare's Globe Theater | 5 |
| Sun Tzu's Art of War | 2 |
| The Colossus | 3 |
| The Great Library | 5 |
| The Great Lighthouse | 2 |
| The Great Wall | 2 |
| The Hanging Gardens | 4 |
| The Manhattan Project | 2 |
| The Oracle | 4 |
| The Pyramids | 4 |
| The United Nations | 4 |
| Theory of Evolution | 3 |
| Universal Suffrage | 4 |

What good is all this culture? It expands the city's cultural *sphere of influence* and contributes to your civilization's overall cultural dominance. We discuss your empire's culture in the next chapter. The sphere of influence is what's important to city management.

The greater a city's culture value, the more area is encompassed by your borders—the spheres of influence. All squares within this border are considered your territory, and you are within your rights to demand that trespassing foreign units get out. Your civilization benefits from any luxuries and strategic resources connected to your cities that fall within your sphere of influence (without the need of a colony). All terrain inside your sphere of influence is always visible to you, regardless of whether you have a unit nearby. Last, but not least, other civilization's units do not enjoy the movement bonuses normally provided by roads and railroads while inside your territory.

It's a good idea to help any city, but especially one near the outside edge of your civilization, enlarge its sphere of influence. Defense is always a priority, but once that's reasonably assured, consider building some of the more civilized improvements. The earlier the better, because the longer an improvement has been around, the greater its effect on your culture.

# Happiness and Civil Disorder

Understanding happiness and its inverse state, civil disorder, is extremely important. The citizens in your cities have one of four different attitudes or emotional states: happiness, contentment, unhappiness, or resistance. The first citizens of your first city start out in a contented state. As the population of the city grows, competition for jobs, commodities, and services increases. Eventually, depending on the difficulty level at which you play and the economic conditions in your city, some citizens start to grumble and display unhappiness. If you don't take an active role in city management as population increases, the natural trend of citizens' attitudes is toward unhappiness.

So what can you do to counter this trend? If your population is already suffering civil disorder because of an attitude imbalance, you need to take immediate steps, as we suggest under "Restoring Order" below. However, you needn't wait until a crisis occurs; you can keep citizens content by taking a longer view and providing services as the demand becomes imminent, or even ahead of demand.

Two special conditions can also cause further unhappiness in your populations. If you're ruling under a representative form of government (Republic or Democracy), *war*

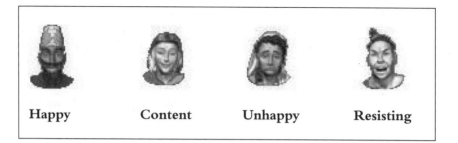

| Happy | Content | Unhappy | Resisting |

*weariness* makes your citizen's unhappy. The more time you spend at war, the more likely your citizens eventually get tired of it. The most important factors in causing war weariness are stationing your units in a rival's territory, enemies having troops in your territory, declaring war, and engaging in battle. Having a rival declare war on you actually decreases war weariness, perhaps because it relieves the prewar uncertainty and tension. In addition, whenever you capture an enemy city, the native population in that city retains its original nationality. Whenever you are at war with their home country, these citizens are likely to become unhappy with you.

## Resistance

Whenever you capture an enemy city, some of the population in that city are likely to resent your rule; they *resist* your occupation of their city. Resistors cannot be assigned to work the terrain. The only way to quell resistance is to station troops in a captured city. With the aid of your troops, over time the resistance will end. Your culture and the type of government affects how fast resistance is tamed.

The tendency to resistance is based on the nationality of the citizens in question. So, for example, if you conquer a Roman city, the Roman citizens are likely to resist. If you recapture one of your cities from the

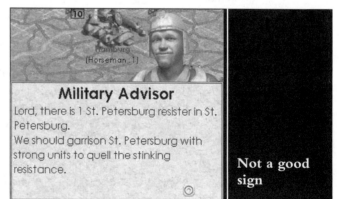

**Military Advisor**

Lord, there is 1 St. Petersburg resister in St. Petersburg.
We should garrison St. Petersburg with strong units to quell the stinking resistance.

**Not a good sign**

Romans, the folks who were previously under your rule won't resist. Any new citizens created after the city was originally taken, however, might resist—because they think of themselves as Romans.

The time it takes resistors to calm down depends on a few factors. A more impressive culture, a government that allows more personal freedom, and a greater supply of luxuries all help. Even after active resistance has ceased, the citizens still retain their nationality for a long time (think of it as a few generations). They are eventually assimilated into your nation entirely, and their nationality changes.

Note that you cannot rush completion of a job if there are any resistors in a city.

## Civil Disorder

As we mentioned earlier in "City Management Concepts," cities that don't maintain a favorable balance of happy people over unhappy people go into civil disorder. Cities in civil disorder *completely* suspend production. A nuclear reactor in a city suffering civil disorder might experience a meltdown due to lax safety controls (see "Nuclear Meltdown" in **Chapter 7: Terrain and Movement**). Keeping a city stable is a very high priority.

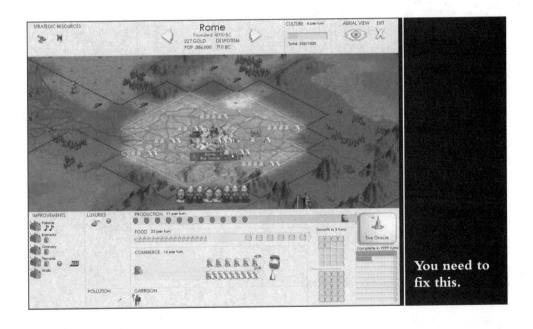

You need to fix this.

A city suffers civil disorder when unhappy people outnumber happy people. Resistors, content people, and Specialists are ignored in the calculation. When order is restored, the city returns to normal operation the next turn. You can restore order in several ways.

## Restoring Order

How do you restore order once a city has gone into civil disorder? Use the same methods by which you keep your populace happy in the first place.

- You can take one or more citizens out of the work force, making them Entertainers. This increases the number of happy people. When creating Specialists, be careful not to also cause shortages of food or resources that trigger starvation of the population or other problems.

- You might be able to connect the city in question to a source of luxury resources. Increasing the availability of luxury resources converts some content people into happy citizens, allowing them to balance the unhappy populace.

- You can go to the Domestic Advisor screen and increase the amount of your per-turn income devoted to providing entertainment to your cities.

- If your civilization operates under Despotism, Monarchy, or Communism, you can use military police to restore order to a city. A small number of military units, each with an attack factor of at least one, can be stationed in a city as military police. Each military unit makes one unhappy citizen in a city content.

# We Love the King Day

If a city's population becomes sufficiently happy, it (not your whole civilization—just this one location) spontaneously holds a celebration in honor of your rule. The people declare a "We Love the King Day" in thanks for the prosperity your management has made possible. While the circumstances that support this celebratory mood continue, the city enjoys certain benefits, depending on your civilization's type of government. You will see the effects of celebration begin on the first *full turn* that a city celebrates (that is, the turn *after* the party is announced).

To trigger a celebration day, a city must fulfill these conditions:

- There can be *no* unhappy citizens in the city.

- There must be at least as many happy citizens as content citizens.

- The population must be at least six.

For example, a city with five happy citizens, four content citizens, and no unhappy citizens celebrates. A city with 10 happy citizens, three content citizens and one unhappy citizen does not.

An ongoing We Love the King Day lowers the levels of corruption and waste, makes the city less likely to defect, and significantly increases the chance of failure if your enemies attempt to initiate propaganda here.

# MANAGING YOUR EMPIRE

*"Roads, mighty armies, and happy citizens—these are the foundations of a strong empire."*

Other than defense, what is important to the overall health and prosperity of your civilization? Answer: a lucrative trade network, scientific research, effective government, a strong culture, and a contented populace.

## Empire Management Concepts

Taking up where we left off last chapter in "City Management Concepts," each city's income from commerce is divided between taxes, entertainment, and science funding.

*Taxes maintain city improvements, support units, and add to your treasury.* Taxes support basic city services and pay the upkeep on your units. Surplus funds accumulate in your treasury. There are plenty of useful ways to spend money, as we've explained elsewhere.

*Entertainment funding increases citizen happiness.* Sometimes you simply need to quell the unhappiness of your citizens. Increasing the percentage of taxes being allocated to entertainment can help turn civil disorder into a peaceful populace.

*Science funding powers your research.* Each new advance requires the accumulation of research to achieve. Each discovery leads to further discoveries, creating a chain of progress. If your cities don't produce much science, your civilization doesn't progress very quickly.

Which is more important: income, entertainment, or research? That depends on what you want to achieve. To give you the most flexibility, the game lets you adjust the proportion of your commerce that's devoted to each. The Science Ratio on the Domestic Advisor's screen lets you change the ratio of taxes to science in 10% increments. The Entertainment Allocation slider lets you change the amount spent on entertainment in 10% increments. The advisor calculates how the new rate affects your funding.

Just one more thing: discovering new advances encompasses more than just new gadgets to improve sanitation and military might. Philosophical concepts and theories are some of your most critical civilization advances. Every civilization starts out under Despotism, but you can develop new forms of government. These might, in turn, have a profound effect on the happiness of your citizens and the rate at which your citizens produce raw materials, food, and commerce.

## Your Trade Network

You know by now that it's helpful to *connect* your cities to luxuries and strategic resources. Now, let's introduce the concept of your civilization's *trade network*.

A city that's connected by road to a strategic resource or luxury (one that's inside your borders or on which you've established a colony) has access to that resource. That city can build the units made possible by the strategic resource, or it enjoys the happiness benefit of that luxury.

Here's the tricky part: any of your cities that are connected to that city are also considered connected to the resource. The connecting road goes through the intervening city after all. (It's the road that counts, not the city.) The network of roads that snake throughout your empire is the basis of your trade network. Of course, each city can only benefit once from each particular type of strategic resource or luxury, but any extras are available for trading with other civilizations.

There's one big caveat about roads. If you are at war with another civilization, any road that passes through your enemy's territory (inside his or her borders) can't be used for the transfer of resources and luxuries. This is not true of peaceful rivals, only those nations with which you are at war. Portions of your trade network can be disconnected by this effect, so be careful and set up alternate routes if possible.

Both these cities are connected to the luxury.

Roads aren't the only way to connect your cities. The Harbor and Airport city improvements act as roads over the sea and through the sky. Any two cities that both have an Airport are considered connected. Two cities that both have a Harbor on the same body of water and an explored sea path between them are also connected. (Sea trading requires the Astronomy advance, and Ocean trading requires Magnetism or Navigation.) These connections are affected by enemy territory.

One last thing deserves mention. You can trade strategic resources and luxuries with other civilizations, but only if their capital is included in a trade network with your capital. That is, your capital cities must be connected to each other.

## Research Rate

When you start a new game, a portion of your income is already dedicated to research. To change the proportions of tax income versus science funding versus entertainment spending, open the Domestic Advisor's screen. Use the [+] and [-] buttons on opposite sides of the Science Ratio bar to move the rate in 10% increments. A notation near the bar lists your treasury's income and outflow per turn. Finally, another entry calculates how many turns it will take to achieve a new advance.

If you are interested in focusing on civilization advances, you might want to increase the amount of scientific research. If you rapidly build city improvements and units, you might want to increase your taxes to cover the maintenance and support costs. Experiment with different rates to see what levels of income and science work well for your style of ruling.

# Entertainment Rate

If your present combination of luxury resources, city improvements, and military police doesn't fulfill your need to make your citizens happy, you might want to increase the amount of income you allocate to providing entertainment to your populace.

To change the proportions of luxury spending versus tax income versus science funding, open the Domestic Advisor's screen. Use the [+] and [-] buttons on opposite sides of the Entertainment Allocation bar to move the rate in 10% increments. A notation near the bar lists your treasury's income and outflow per turn. Finally, another entry notes how many "happy faces" the current level of funding creates.

# Corruption

Your commerce income from any city is affected by *corruption*, much as production is lowered by waste. When an empire sprawls over a wide area, corruption lowers the total tax intake in cities on the fringes and frontiers. The more sophisticated the government and the smaller the sprawl, the less effect corruption has. Building certain city

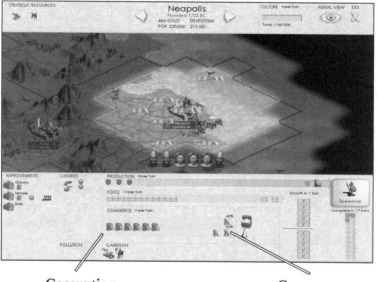

Corruption                                    Commerce

improvements, completing the Small Wonder Forbidden Palace, and switching to a more advanced form of government can counteract this loss.

## War Weariness

It's a truism that in war the peasants suffer the most. When you continually wage war, your citizenry eventually get tired of it. This effect is known as *war weariness*. Under representative governments (Republic and Democracy), when your citizens feel free to express their distaste for military action, war weariness causes great unhappiness in your cities.

A few factors cause increased war weariness. The most important ones are stationing your units in enemy territory, enemies having troops in your territory, declaring war, and engaging in battle. Having a rival declare war on you actually decreases war weariness, perhaps because it relieves the prewar uncertainty and tension.

## Governments

Another vital management tool is the type of government under which you operate your civilization. Every civilization starts out as a Despotism, but some of the advances you can research are intellectual in nature, rather than technological, and these include governmental concepts. Once you have discovered a new form of government, you can choose to support a revolution in order to change government types.

Anarchy, or the lack of government, occurs only when you lose control—either because you've called for a revolution or civil unrest has toppled the current regime. Civil unrest continues as long as conditions are ripe for it. In both cases, your people's attitude naturally stabilizes. After a few turns, once your civilization settles down, a dialog box appears listing

**Domestic Advisor**

Sir, our people yearn for a change in government to
Monarchy.
Shall we encourage a revolution?

○ Tell me more about governments.

○ Yes, let the revolt begin!

○ No. We are happy with *Despotism*.

all the possible forms of government your culture has available. Choose the one you like, and that regime takes effect immediately.

There are five forms of government: Despotism, Monarchy, the Republic, Communism, and Democracy. (Depending on your style of play, you might not develop the governments in order of sophistication.) The Republic and Democracy are the most sophisticated from an economic point of view, but they impose severe restrictions on your military forces. The other forms offer trade-offs between economics, cultural freedom, and increased military flexibility. In essence, you could summarize governmental variants this way: the more freedom you give your people, the less they will want to fight for you, but the stronger your economy becomes.

Resistors in any captured city are eventually mollified (especially if your culture is more impressive than their former nation's), but the difference between the city's old and new governments can affect the time it takes. Generally, if the conqueror's form of government is more advanced, the better overall quality of life helps persuade the resistors to face the inevitable earlier. On the other hand, resistors living under a less advanced form of government are even less enthusiastic to be integrated into the new culture.

A similar effect applies to propaganda. If your government offers more personal freedom and economic promise than that of the civilization from which you're attempting to lure away a city, your chances of success are better.

## Anarchy

Your civilization is in a temporary state of having no central government at all. You continue controlling the movements of your units, and your cities continue to operate on their own, but some important functions of your civilization grind to a halt until control is restored.

**Military police:** You cannot use military force to quell civil disorder under Anarchy.

**Corruption and waste:** Corruption is catastrophic—so much so that, while no maintenance is charged for city improvements, no tax revenue is collected either.

**Production:** Your cities produce absolutely nothing except food for as long as Anarchy persists. None of the usual methods of hurrying production are available.

**Science:** Since there is no income to apportion, no scientific research is accomplished while Anarchy continues. You also can adjust your Science Rate but it has no effect.

**Support:** Your units, both military and non-military, require no gold for support.

**Special conditions:**

- While Anarchy continues, citizens cannot work up to potential. The penalty for this atmosphere of tension is that workers produce one fewer food in any terrain that can generate more than two.

- Your Workers' lack of motivation means that they toil 50% slower than usual.

# Despotism

You rule by absolute fiat. The people just have to live with it because your will is enforced by the military. Due to the severe limits on economic and personal freedom, production is at a minimum. But total control makes conducting war relatively easy.

**Military police:** Up to two troops in each city can keep the peace; each makes one unhappy citizen content (see "Happiness and Civil Disorder" in **Chapter 11: Managing Your Cities**).

**Corruption and waste:** Corruption and waste are both rampant under Despotism. Commerce losses due to corruption and shield production losses due to waste increase with the distance a city is located from its capital and the number of cities in your civilization.

**Production:** You can hurry production of a city's current project for no monetary cost, but the coercion involved alienates the populace, and many people find ways to leave. The project gets done, but as a result, the city's population drops.

**Resource support:** Under Despotism, your iron rule allows you to command four units for each town, city, and metropolis without paying support. Each unit in excess of this requires one gold each turn.

**Special conditions:**

- Citizens cannot work up to their potential. If a terrain produces more than two, the maximum production of food, shields, and commerce is reduced by one, regardless of what the terrain might normally produce.

- In the event of a military emergency, you can draft two units of citizenry per city to create infantry units. Of course, this normally causes some resentment among the remaining populace.

- A *town* has a population of 6 or lower.

- It becomes a *city* when the population is from 7 to 12.

- Above population 12, it's a *metropolis*.

# Monarchy

Your rule is less than absolute, and an aristocracy of upper-class citizens influences your decisions. The aristocratic classes, at least, have a certain amount of economic freedom, and this results in the potential for greater production. Your feudal vassals are partially responsible for helping to defend your kingdom, but they may in some cases deduct a share of your civilization's production as maintenance for military units.

**Military police:** Up to three troops in each city can acts as military police, each one making one unhappy citizen content (see "Happiness and Civil Disorder" in the previous chapter).

**Corruption and waste:** Your aristocrats, particularly those farthest from your watchful eye, siphon off a certain amount of your economic output. Corruption and waste are significant problems under Monarchy, though not as severe as under Despotism. Commerce income lost due to corruption and shield production losses due to waste increase with the distance a city is located from its capital.

**Production:** You can pay to hurry production of a city's current project.

**Resource support:** Your feudal vassals support up to two units for each town under your rule, four for each city, and eight for each metropolis. Each unit over and above that total costs one gold per turn.

**Special conditions:**

- In the event of a military emergency, you can draft two citizens per city per turn to create infantry units. Of course, this normally causes some resentment among the remaining populace.

# Republic

You rule over an assembly of city-states formed from the cities that your civilization controls. Each city is an autonomous state, yet also is part of the republic that you rule. The people feel that you rule at their request. They enjoy substantial personal and economic freedom, and this results in greatly increased tax income. Military conflict is unpopular among the masses, and your government must bear the full cost of supporting its army.

**Military police:** No troops can act as military police.

**Corruption and waste:** Corruption and waste remain a nuisance under a Republic, though they're not nearly as severe as they are under a Monarchy. Commerce losses due to corruption and shield production losses due to waste increase with the distance a city is located from its capital. Corruption and waste also increase with the number of cities in your civilization.

**Production:** You can pay to hurry production of a city's current project.

**Resource support:** Your citizens support no free units. Each unit requires one gold for support each turn.

**Special conditions:**

- Under a Republic, your workers produce one extra commerce in any square where they were already producing at least one.

- In the event of a military emergency, you can draft only one unit of citizenry per city per turn to create an infantry unit. This still causes resentment among the remaining populace.

- War weariness (described earlier in this chapter) has a profound negative effect on your citizens' happiness.

# Communism

You are the head of a communist government, and you rule with the support of the controlling party. Although this form of government allows more production than Despotism, the orthodoxy of the party restricts personal and economic freedom, limiting tax income. On the positive side, corruption is negated by the action of the local party apparatus, the army and secret police suppress most dissent, and your large security forces recruit excellent spies.

**Military police:** Up to four troops in each city can enforce martial law; each makes one unhappy citizen content (see "Happiness and Civil Disorder" in **Chapter 11: Managing Your Cities**).

**Corruption and waste:** Corruption and waste are a problem under Communism, but less than that experienced by a Monarchy. State control of the economy does standardize the loss of commerce and shields—so that distance from your capital has no effect. Corruption and waste also increase with the number of cities in your civilization.

**Production:** You can hurry production of a city's current project without financial cost, but the repressive policies required alienate the populace, and many people decide to emigrate. The project gets done, but as a result, the city's population drops.

**Resource support:** Your centralized military-industrial complex can support two units from each town, four from each city, and eight from each metropolis at no cost to you. Each unit over and above that requires one gold per turn.

**Special conditions:**

*   Under a Communist government, espionage missions have a greater chance of success.

*   In the event of a military emergency, you can draft two citizens per city per turn to create infantry units. This causes resentment among the remaining populace.

## Democracy

You rule as the elected executive of a modern Democracy. The people feel that you rule because they chose you. The degree of freedom allowed under this government results in the maximum opportunity for economic production and tax income. However, the people also have a very strong voice in determining how much economic production is devoted to improving the standard of living. Maintaining a military force in the field comes with great political and economic costs.

**Military police:** No troops can act as military police.

**Corruption and waste:** One of Democracy's greatest advantages is its ability to squelch corruption and waste. Both are minimal in your cities.

**Production:** You can pay to hurry production of a city's current project.

**Resource support:** Your citizens support no free units. Each unit requires one gold for support each turn.

**Special Conditions:**

- Under a Democracy, your citizens generate one additional commerce in any square where they're already producing at least one.

- Patriotism and strong democratic traditions make your cities completely immune to propaganda.

- Your Workers, highly motivated by the free enterprise system, work 50% faster than usual.

- In the event of a military emergency, you can draft one citizen per city to create an infantry unit. This causes quite a bit of resentment among the remaining populace.

- War weariness (described earlier in this chapter) has a profound negative effect on your citizens' happiness. In fact, if you remain at war for too long, your Democracy can fall into anarchy.

# Culture

We discuss how to create and strengthen each city's culture in **Chapter 11: Managing Your Cities**. What we're concerned with here is your civilization's overall cultural rating and its effects. The combined culture points that all your cities accumulate make up your total culture rating. Modifying this are several factors, including your scientific progress and form of government.

When you capture a city from another civilization, it takes the people in that city time to stop resisting your rule and even longer to assimilate into your culture and become nationalized. The time it takes depends (among other things) on whether your culture is more or less impressive than that of their home nation. A strong culture significantly shortens the wait.

When you enter into diplomatic negotiations, the other ruler's opinion of and attitude toward you are affected by the relative strengths of your cultures. If your civilization's culture is impressive enough, a positive relationship is easier to establish and to maintain.

Finally, as we've mentioned elsewhere, a culture can be so thoroughly dominant that enemy cities long to be a part of it. It is even possible for a city that lies near the sphere of influence of another to be overcome by the sheer weight of the cultural imbalance and switch sides without provocation.

# Nationality

One concept that has been touched on but not really explained is the *nationality* of citizens and units. It's pretty much what it sounds like; your citizens and units (and those of other nations) know and remember what civilization they were born into. Let's explain this by example.

Say you're ruling the Greeks. Any citizen in any of your cities is a *Greek* citizen. All of your units, military and otherwise, are *Greek* units. Simple enough—until cities and units start trading hands.

If you capture a Worker from your neighbors, the Americans, that Worker is yours to command, but it's still an *American* Worker. The unit retains its nationality. Whenever you negotiate trades with the American ruler, he or she is likely to ask for the return of any American Workers you have under your control. All of this goes for any captured units, including Settlers.

What about cities? Let's say the French tick you off, so just to teach them a lesson, you march right over and invade Rouen. The city is yours (for the moment); it's a *Greek* city. The citizens of Rouen, however, know darn well that they're *French*, not Greek. Thus, you have a city full of Frenchmen under your control. Some of them might be resistors. In time, you can convince resistors to calm down and work for you, but they'll still be *French*.

If you keep Rouen for a while, the city will grow. Any new citizens created under your rule are *Greek* citizens. So the population of Rouen could be a peaceful mix of nationalities. Another way to make Greek citizens is the sheer pressure of time. After a number of turns (think of it as several generations), *French* citizens can be assimilated and become *Greek* citizens. How long this takes depends on a few factors, especially the relative strengths of your cultures.

It's a different situation if the French take Rouen by force. Just as some of the *French* citizens became resistors when you invaded, so the *Greek* citizens can become resistors when the French retake the city. Any remaining *French* citizens in Rouen will not resist; they're perfectly happy to be returned to their nation of birth.

# 13
# DIPLOMACY AND TRADE

*"You cannot please everyone, but if you rule the routes of trade and have the world by the throat, it matters less."*

Other cultures share your world. If your attitude is expansionist and your home continent is large, you might seek out and find your rivals early in the game. If you concentrate on perfecting your own cities or find yourself limited by a small continent, it might be centuries before you encounter other civilizations. Whether you opt for peaceful communications or aggressive action depends on your style. This chapter describes the essentials of diplomacy and of carrying on trade with your neighbors.

## Concepts of Diplomacy

Eventually, no matter how remote your location or how isolationist your policies, you will have contact with rival civilizations. Once you make contact with a rival, you can speak to them at any time by right-clicking one of their units, using the Diplomacy button on the Info Box, or calling up the Foreign Advisor and clicking the picture of that leader.

Every one of your opponents has an *attitude* that he or she presents during negotiations. Your rivals' attitudes can range from enthusiastically friendly to furiously hostile.

The leader's attitude toward you is noted beneath his or her likeness during negotiations. Rulers also have personality traits that affect their attitudes. Your rivals' attitudes change over time, depending on your rank in the game, the current balance of power, the gifts you offer them, and your *reputation* for keeping your word in negotiations. Every time you go back on your word, international observers notice and remember.

You are naturally at peace with all your rivals at the start of the game, and you can strengthen the bond by trading advances, luxuries, strategic resources, and gold. If you build an embassy in a rival's capital, you can enter into diplomatic agreements to allow each other access to your territories and transportation infrastructures, and you can ally against third parties. A rival might demand money, civilization advances, or other gifts in exchange for any treaty—or just to prevent him from attacking you. (You can demand tribute for *your* goodwill, too.) In addition, negotiations can include requests to share maps and instructions to withdraw trespassing troops. A ruler might even ask you to declare war on a third party. All negotiations progress through the Diplomacy screen.

# Conducting Diplomacy

You conduct diplomacy on the Diplomacy screen, which offers you an array of options.

When you meet with a rival ruler, your advisors are at your shoulder (in the upper right corner of the Diplomacy screen), feeding you whatever details they have that seem relevant and helpful in the current situation. Pay attention; they can give you the advantage you need in a tense negotiation. You can click More to get further advice.

If you have an embassy in their capital, it is a valuable source of information about that civilization. With an embassy, you can learn about your opponent's diplomatic connections with others; you'll find this intelligence on the Foreign Advisor's report. The Military Advisor gets a complete list of their forces from an embassy.

## Mood and Personality

The tone and result of any negotiations are greatly influenced by the mood of your rival (which is noted on the Diplomacy screen). The opposing leader might be furious, annoyed, cautious, polite, or gracious. His or her mood depends on personality and

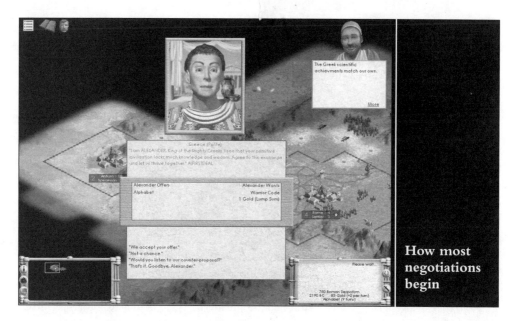

how your two civilizations compare to each other and to the rest of the world—
plus how you've been treating each other.

The other leaders' basic personalities are as varied as their cultures: arrogant, aggressive,
reasonable, expansionist, isolationist, artistic, decadent, overconfident, perfectionist,
cautious. You'll encounter them all at some point. Your rivals, like human beings
throughout history, will not always act rationally. They might start wars on the slightest
pretext or demand exorbitant payments for peace treaties. Sometimes they're bluffing.

If you have broken agreements with any civilization, your perfidy is remembered and
influences everyone's opinion of you.

## Reputation

Your reputation is based not on how peaceful or how warlike you are toward your
neighbors, but on how often you keep your word. Breaking alliances or treaties can
blacken your reputation in the international community. Savagely razing the city of an
enemy or using a right of passage agreement to set up Cannons to bombard your opponent's cities are acts likely to be deplored throughout the known world. Espionage,
whether successful of not, can also damage your standing.

Your opponents learn from your actions and adjust theirs to fit their expectations. If you habitually break treaties, other leaders will have no qualms about doing the same to you. Over long periods of time, if you mend your ways by keeping your word to other rulers, the black marks on your reputation can be partially erased and your honor somewhat redeemed. Only through this effect can a leader who has broken his or her word regain a spotless reputation.

# Embassies

After you've established communications with another civilization *and* discovered Writing, you can set up an embassy. Your diplomats establish official contact with the selected leader and set up an office in his or her capital city. You can also investigate your rival's cities and attempt to steal civilization advances.

As already mentioned, establishing embassies with other civilizations gives your advisors access to plenty of new information. Your Foreign Advisor will know a *lot* more about a civilization with which you have an embassy. In addition, your Military Advisor can investigate your rivals through the embassy and get a complete list of their forces.

## Establishing an Embassy

To establish an embassy, double-click the Foreign Ministry icon on your capital city. A menu opens, listing the civilizations you have contacted, are not at war with, and do not already have an embassy with. The cost in gold of establishing an embassy with each nation is listed in the menu. Select the rival in whose capital you want the embassy.

It is only necessary to establish an embassy once with any particular civilization. Even if you manage to get it closed down (through war with that civilization), it

> **FOREIGN MINISTRY**
> Establish an embassy with whom?
>
> ⚪ Russia (24 gold)
>
>                         ◎ X

reopens when peace is declared. Note that your advisors won't be able to collect their extra information during the war—unless you have a Spy (more about that later in this chapter).

## Diplomatic Actions

As soon as the embassy is in action, you have the option to use it. Your diplomats act as ambassadors, envoys, and information gatherers. You can either investigate the rival's capital city (with no chance of failure or incident) or examine your Foreign Advisor's report on the civilization, based on the newly uncovered information.

In the future, you can double-click the embassy icon on your rival's capital city to open the menu of the possible diplomatic activities. (Be aware that enemies can use all the same techniques against your civilization as you use against theirs.)

**Investigate a city:** Your diplomatic corps gathers information about the rival city you select. When they've completed their research, you see that city's City Display. You can examine what armies are defending the city and what improvements have been built there. When you exit the City Display, you return to the Map window. (When you first establish the embassy, you can investigate the enemy's capital without risk or penalty.)

**Steal a technology:** Your diplomats attempt to steal one civilization advance from the rival civilization. There are three levels of caution you can instruct them to use. The more money you allow them to spend, the greater their chances of success and of escaping discovery.

# The Diplomatic States

There are several possible diplomatic states and agreements. In one sense, the relationship between two nations can be expressed as one of two different states: peace or war. War is relatively straightforward. When you are at peace with another civilization (the natural state when you first meet a rival), there are multiple possibilities for deals and lasting agreements. Each of the potential agreements you can make has repercussions on both parties' actions, the movement and position of units, and the international reputations of the participants. A short description of each agreement and state follows.

## Peace

A peace treaty is, in theory, a permanent arrangement. You and your rival agree not to attack each other or even enter the other's territory with military units. A ruler's territory encompasses any space within the spheres of influence (borders) of his or her cities. Units that violate this agreement may be asked to leave—and their failure to do so immediately can be considered a treaty violation.

Peace treaties are most useful when you want a long period of quiet on a particular border, since their recognition of territorial borders keeps enemy units from harassing you and fortifying near your cities. By the same token, they impede you from entrenching your units in your treaty partner's territory. A peace treaty, when combined with an embassy, also opens up negotiations to several other agreements and, just as importantly, makes trade with the other civilization possible.

## Military Alliance

Once you have an embassy with a friendly nation, you can sign a military alliance against a common enemy. This type of alliance lasts for 20 turns. At the end of that period, either party can cancel the agreement with no hard feelings. Leaving the military alliance won't cancel the state of war with the third party, of course. That has to be taken care of in separate negotiations. On the other hand, if either party to the alliance makes peace with the third party, it effectively destroys the alliance.

Breaking an alliance for any reason is remembered as a major transgression by all of the other civilizations. If you sign a peace treaty with the third party or, even worse, attack your ally, your reputation suffers a black mark that is only very slowly erased by time. To cancel an alliance without getting a black mark, you must wait for its natural expiration date to do so.

## Right of Passage

You can sign a right of passage if you have an embassy with a friendly nation. In a right of passage agreement, your two civilizations agree to let each other's units pass freely through each other's territory. This includes the ability to use (and enjoy the movement bonuses of) each other's roads and railroads. That's the extent of the agreement.

A right of passage agreement lasts for 20 turns. At the end of that period, either party can cancel the agreement without consequences. Using a right of passage to infiltrate your troops for a surprise attack is remembered as a cold-hearted breach of trust by all of the other civilizations. If you attack your ally, your reputation takes a nose dive and you'll find it difficult, if not impossible, to get anyone to trust you in the near future. To cancel a right of passage without trouble, wait for its natural expiration.

## Trade Embargo

If you have discovered Nationalism and have an embassy, you can arrange a trade embargo with an ally. This is an agreement not to trade strategic resources or luxuries with a specific third party. A trade embargo is not a declaration of war, though it's sometimes enough of an affront to inspire one.

The cooperative embargo lasts for 20 turns. At the end of that period, either party can cancel the embargo with a clear conscience.

## Mutual Protection Pact

If a peace treaty and embassy are in place between two civilizations and either has discovered Nationalism, they can negotiate a mutual protection pact. This is an agreement that each will come to the other's aid in case of attack by any third party. That is, your ally expects your military assistance if he or she is attacked, and you should expect the same from his or her forces.

The pact lasts for 20 turns. At the end of that period, either party can cancel the agreement with no repercussions. Leaving the mutual protection pact won't cancel a state of war with any third party. That has to be taken care of in separate negotiations.

Violating a mutual protection pact is seen as a major breach of trust by all of the other civilizations. If you make peace with a civilization while it is still invading your ally, your reputation suffers for quite some time. To cancel a pact without consequences, you must wait for it to expire.

# War

This diplomatic state represents the likelihood of open hostilities at any point in which your units contact your opponent's units.

Wars can start for innumerable reasons, ranging from self-defense to greed and conquest. War might be openly declared after a breakdown

**Foreign Advisor**
We have declared war on the Russians.

Now you've done it.

in negotiations or in return for offenses rendered by ill-placed troops, or it can start with a sudden sneak attack. Civilizations at war with yours might drag their neighbors into the conflict, too, by activating mutual protection pacts or forming military alliances against you.

Once you are at war with another civilization, that ruler considers you a hated enemy unless and until you manage to negotiate a peace treaty. You must make peace separately with each opponent (even those allied with a civilization with whom you have already negotiated peace). If, for instance, the Romans and the Greeks were allies in a war against you, you must negotiate one agreement to end hostilities with the Greeks and a separate one to placate the Romans.

# Trade Agreements

If you want to set up ongoing commerce with another civilization, you must do it explicitly during negotiations. If your capital cities are connected (as described under "Your Trade Network" in **Chapter 12: Managing Your Empire**), you and the other leaders can trade strategic resources—a great way to get access to a resource you don't have in your territory. You can also set up a trade in luxuries for a temporary boost in your citizens' happiness. All trade agreements last 20 turns before coming up for review (unless war cuts them off).

# Negotiations

To begin negotiations with another ruler, you must first make contact with that civilization. You make first contact whenever one of your units crosses paths with one of theirs. You can also trade with leaders you have already met to gain communications with those you haven't if the leader you're bargaining with has made contact with them (see "Making a Proposal" below for the details). After communications are set up, they're never lost. You can contact the leader in a few ways:

- Right-click any one of the leader's units, then select the Contact (unit) option.

- Open the Foreign Advisor's screen and double-click the portrait of the leader you want to contact.

- Press [Shift]-[D].

- Click on the Diplomacy button in the Unit Info box.

- Move one of your units into the other nation's territory and wait for them to contact you (not recommended unless your intention is to annoy your rival).

If you are at war with the leader you attempt to contact, he or she might refuse to meet with you or make demands that you must satisfy if you wish to progress in your negotiations. Again, the options available to you depend on the situation. They're all worded so as to be self-explanatory, but if negotiations involve a trade proposal or counterproposal (and they almost invariably do), you'll need to know how the proposal process works.

## Making a Proposal

Once you have your rival's ear, you can make a great variety of offers. Common sense tells you that the more an opponent likes you, the more likely he or she is to agree to your proposal. Opponents also take your relative standing in the game into account. They are more likely to be magnanimous if you are far behind than if you're the preeminent power in the world.

Your rivals will often come to the table with a particular deal in mind. They'll request something from you and offer something (even if it's only a vague assurance that they might not attack you) in exchange. Your options include accepting the deal as offered, bluntly rejecting the exchange, or offering a counterproposal instead of the deal they requested. They, in turn, can accept or decline your revised offer. Sometimes an opponent thinks less of you for offering lesser alternatives. You may continue trading as long as there are items to trade and the other party is interested.

When you choose to make a proposal or counterproposal to the leader on the other side of the negotiating table, the Diplomacy screen expands to include the necessary tools—the Negotiation Panels:

- **Possible requests:** The column on the left lists everything you might want to ask the rival leader to give you.

- **Possible offers:** The right-hand column lists what you have to offer the other leader.

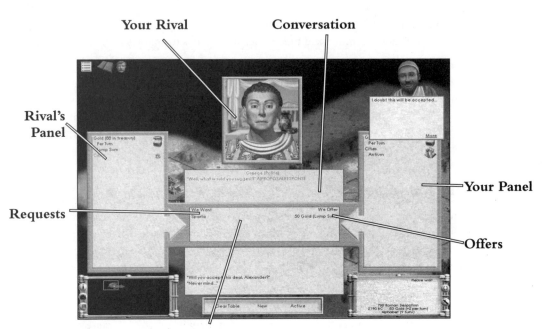

**Your Rival** **Conversation**

**Rival's Panel**

**Requests**

**Your Panel**

**Offers**

**The Table**

What categories are listed on each side depends on the current situation. Here are all the categories that might appear:

- **Peace treaty:** Peace treaties open the door to other diplomatic agreements. This option is only available if you are at war with the rival you're dealing with. In fact, it's the only diplomatic agreement that appears during a war, since it's a condition of the other agreements.

- **Diplomatic agreements:** When you offer to enter into a diplomatic agreement (the possible agreements were described earlier), you'll notice that it appears on both sides of the offer table. That's because all these agreements are mutual—you both agree to do the same thing for each other.

- **Trade embargoes:** When you don't wish to declare war on a rival, but still feel a need to inhibit his progress, you can agree with another civilization that you'll both refuse to trade with that rival for 20 turns. Even allies, however, are likely to ask for some compensation for the loss of trade. Of course, this also doesn't do much for the embargoed party's opinion of you.

- **Communications:** Contact with another civilization is valuable, and nearly anything with value can be offered in trade. When one side of a negotiation has made contact with a nation that the other side has not yet met, communications with that third party can be shared as part of a deal.

- **Maps:** Civilizations might agree to exchange knowledge of the world in the form of accurate maps. If you receive a map in trade, the darkness is rolled back in your Map window to include the new information. The *World Map* includes all the territory the nation has explored or found out about from others, including terrain improvements, city locations, and city sizes. The *Territory Map* gives only the outlines of your borders (cities' cultural spheres of influence).

- **Luxuries:** If a leader has access to a luxury (as described in **Chapter 7: Terrain and Movement**), it can be traded. If you receive a luxury in trade, all your cities that are connected to your capital (see "Your Trade Network" in the previous chapter) have access to it and enjoy the happiness benefit for the duration of the agreement. Like all trade agreements, a luxuries deal lasts for 20 turns or until interrupted by war between the parties to the trade.

- **Strategic resources:** When a civilization has access to a strategic resource, it can be traded. If you receive a resource in trade, all your cities that are connected to your capital (see "Your Trade Network" in the previous chapter) have access to it and can build items that require it for the duration of the agreement. Like all trade agreements, a resources deal lasts for 20 turns or until interrupted by war between the parties to the trade.

- **Gold:** Offering a portion of the contents of your treasury is one of the more convincing negotiating tactics. The Lump Sum option makes a one-time transfer of a specified amount. Be careful with the Per Turn option; it commits a leader to pay the specified amount *every turn* for the next 20 turns. Only the outbreak of war between the trading parties interrupts the required payments.

- **Technology:** Any civilization advance that one nation has discovered or acquired but the other hasn't and can research is a potential item of trade. Knowledge is a particularly valuable asset, and not to be traded lightly or cheaply. As soon as you get an advance in trade, it is as if you had discovered it yourself. (If you trade for the advance your researchers are working on, your Science Advisor will ask you for a new project.)

- **Cities:** As cities are the heart of any civilization, under normal circumstances a leader would rather go to war than trade one away. The option to trade cities exists, however, and can be useful—especially if you need to mollify a particularly aggressive and powerful neighbor.

- **Workers:** Any Worker currently in your capital city can be offered for trade. The same goes for workers in your rival's capital. A traded Worker retains its nationality, just like a captured one.

Click on any category to expand it into a list of specific items; click again if you want to conceal the list. Anything that the leader on the opposite side of the table doesn't need doesn't appear. (For example, an advance you've already discovered won't show up on the left.) Items that one or the other of you has but can't offer at present are grayed out. When you find an item you want to put on the table, click it.

## What's on the Table

At the bottom center of the Diplomacy screen during trade negotiations is the Negotiating Table. This is where the current offer, the deal as it stands, is displayed. Below the table are three handy buttons:

- **Clear:** This button clears everything off the table and lets you start fresh.

- **Active:** Click this button to review your current status and ongoing deals with this leader. Everything that you've already agreed on is set out on the table.

- **New:** When you're looking at what deals are active, click this to return the display on the Proposal Table to the negotiation at hand.

As soon as there is at least one item on the table, new options start appearing in the Diplomacy screen:

- **Ask acceptance:** When there are items on both sides of the table and you think the terms of the deal are fair enough that your rival might accept, you can make the proposal. Once you've done so, be aware that if he or she accepts, the deal is done. Click this option only when you're sure that the deal is one you're willing to abide by.

- **Offer a gift:** If anything is on your side of the table, but your rival's side is empty, you can offer your items as gifts, asking nothing in exchange. If you'd like to improve an opponent's attitude toward you, giving gifts is one of the surest ways.

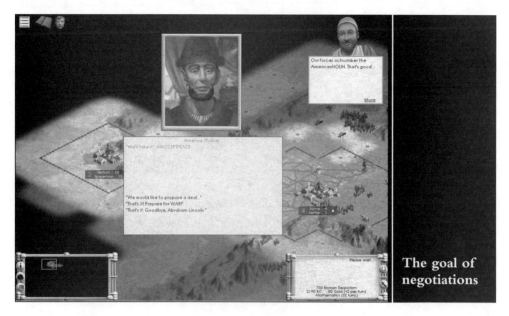

The goal of negotiations

- **Make me an offer:** Rather than giving away what's on your side of the table, you can ask the other leader what he or she is willing to trade for it. You can confidently expect them to bid low, but this is a good way to find out if what they're willing to pay is even close to what you consider reasonable.

- **What can I trade you:** If the other leader has something specific that you're interested in, you can put it on the table yourself and ask what he or she would want in trade for it. Your rival will look at what you have available and make a bid. Of course, the starting bid might or might not be the only deal acceptable to the other leader.

- **Demand tribute:** If you're in an unassailable position of power, you might want to dispense with politeness and just demand what you want. You can also use this as a bluffing tactic, to convince the other leader that you're more powerful or threatening than you actually are. Don't expect it to always work, though. This is one of the more effective ways of making the other leader dislike you. In fact, demanding tribute is a good way to incite a declaration of war.

# Espionage

After you've developed Espionage and built the Intelligence Agency, your embassies become much more powerful tools. They can now be ordered to try to *Plant a Spy* for you (at a cost, of course). If this act is successful, it gives you the potential to undertake a greater range of covert activities. (If it fails—you guessed it—international incident.)

## Covert Actions

Once your Spy is in place, the flow of information is not interrupted during a war, even though your embassy itself might be closed for the duration. In addition, your Military Advisor not only knows the extent of your rival's military forces, but the Spy gives him their *locations* as well.

Your Spy can also undertake a greater range of covert activities than your diplomats can.

**Sabotage:** Carefully maneuvering in the back streets, your agents manage to infiltrate the selected city and gain access to a critical organization or defensive structure. They'll destroy half of the shields already accumulated for the current project.

**Propaganda:** Your operatives contact dissidents within a city and provide resources to spread disinformation, rumors, and other propaganda aimed at convincing the city's populace that they'd be better off as part of your civilization. If the effort is successful, the city revolts and joins your civilization. Cities of a Democracy are immune to propaganda. Enemy capitals and cities with Courthouses are less likely to revolt. Also, it is easier to push a city already in civil disorder into open revolt than it is to undermine a contented city.

**Plant disease:** Your Spy can be ordered to poison the water supply of one of your rival's cities. A successful attempt reduces the target city's population.

**Steal plans:** Stealthily burglarizing the Military Advisor's headquarters, your agent acquires the latest strategic reports. For the remainder of the turn, you know the positions of all of that rival's troops.

**Steal World Map:** Infiltrating the Palace, your agent sneaks into the map room and copies the rival ruler's World Map.

**Expose Spy:** Temporarily reassigned to your capital, your agent pursues a sophisticated counterintelligence program, ferreting out and exposing a rival's Spy. Of course, your rivals can expose your operatives, too.

## Counterespionage

How can you or your rivals prevent these unfriendly acts of espionage? If you suspect that another civilization has managed to plant a Spy, you can make an attempt to *expose* their operative. A Spy is required before espionage activities can be attempted, so successful exposure prevents espionage—at least until another Spy is inserted.

To expose an enemy Spy, you must successfully plant a Spy of your own in their capital. Then, use the Expose Spy option (described above, in "Covert Actions"). If you're successful, the enemy Spy is caught red-handed and disgraced. Of course, your rival could always plant another…

## International Incidents

Whenever you attempt any covert diplomatic action, including the acts of espionage described earlier, there is a chance of discovery. Discovery invariably results in an international incident. Note that the chance of your treachery being discovered is distinct and separate from your odds of success. You can succeed and still spark an incident.

If your attempt is exposed, whether it was successful or not, the targeted civilization is likely to treat your treachery as an act of war. (A target with which you are good friends, though, might sometimes choose to disregard your act.)

# WINNING THE GAME

*"I never for a moment lose sight of my divine mission. Everything else is a means to that end."*

As mentioned in **Chapter 2: Introduction**, you can win the game in several different ways. Depending on what rules you chose to play by (see **Chapter 3: Setting Up a Game** for details), you can beat the other civilizations by being the first to successfully complete the spaceship for the voyage to Alpha Centauri, conquering all the other civilizations in the game, dominating the world, becoming Secretary-General of the United Nations, or proving your cultural dominance.

## Spaceship to Alpha Centauri

The environmental pressures of growing populations in the modern world are forcing humans to look into space for resources and room to live. The question is not whether humans will travel to the stars, but when. The final act of stewardship you can perform for your civilization is to ensure that they lead this exodus.

In the original *Civilization* game, the one non-military method of winning was to construct an interstellar colony ship and send it to successfully land on a planet in the Alpha Centauri system. While it's no longer the only peaceful method, it's still a project that can lead to victory.

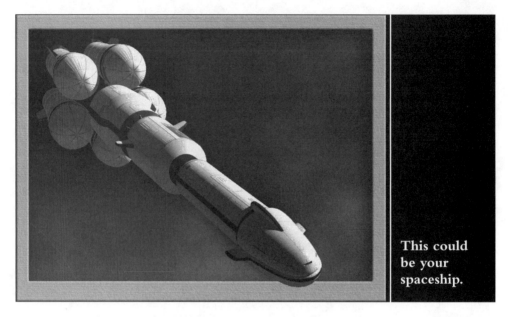

This could
be your
spaceship.

Even if it has developed the necessary technology, no civilization can undertake construction of spaceship components until it has completed the necessary Small Wonder: the Apollo Program.

A spaceship is in many ways a one-shot deal. Each civilization, including yours, can build only one at a time. You can construct a second spaceship only if your current one is destroyed—that is, if your capital city is captured while your ship is under construction (the conquerors destroy it on the launch pad).

The competition ends when either you or one of your opponents launches a spaceship to Alpha Centauri with colonists. The civilization that wins the race to launch wins the game.

## Constructing a Spaceship

Your interstellar colonization project is such a large undertaking that it cannot be built whole-cloth the way improvements are built. It is, instead, constructed of 10 parts, or components. You must achieve specific civilization advances to make components available for construction. The delivery of parts to your assembly and launch facility is handled automatically, however, as each part is completed.

The purpose of your spaceship is to carry colonists to another star system. As each new component is completed, the Spaceship display appears, showing where the component is positioned and updating the statistics and specifications. When all 10 components are complete and in place, you're ready for liftoff. Your launch crews assemble, complete the pre-launch checks, and send your spaceship on its voyage.

# Dominating the World

History has shown that becoming the *de facto* ruler of the world doesn't necessarily mean conquering every square mile. If the vast majority of the world's land and population are inside your borders, your dominance is assured. You can win the game by achieving this sort of domination.

# Conquering Your Rivals

You can also win a military victory by completely overrunning every other civilization in the game. The object is to totally conquer any and all rival civilizations. If at any time you are the only civilization left standing, you're proclaimed ruler of the world.

# Diplomatic Triumph

An option that's new in this *Civilization III* game is winning the game based on diplomacy. It's possible to wheel and deal your way to success, though that doesn't mean military actions become unnecessary. When the United Nations convenes, you must be elected Secretary-General by a vote of the majority of all the civilizations in the world—then your hegemony is assured.

# Cultural Victory

Another new road to success is through cultural dominance. When a culture is so overwhelmingly impressive and widespread that even the rulers of other civilizations long to take part in it, it can be said that that civilization truly controls the world, regardless of the military and political situation.

Your empire's culture score is the total of all your cities' culture points. If your civilization manages to accumulate enough culture points, your culture is dominant and you win the game. See the Civilopedia for more detail.

# Histographic Victory

Every turn, the game calculates your current score, based primarily on the amount of territory within your borders and your content and happy citizens (including Specialists). This score is charted for you in the Histograph screen. The average of all these per-turn totals is your overall Civilization Score. If no one wins in any of the other ways before the last year of the game, the Histographic winner is the ruler with the highest overall score.

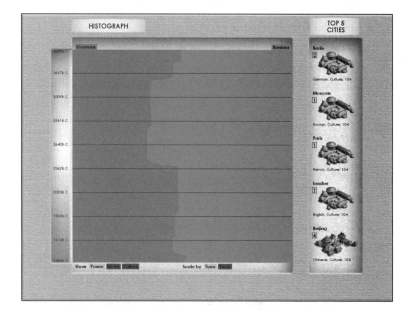

# REFERENCE: SCREEN BY SCREEN

*"Every detail—the bending of a branch, the shift in the path of a bird—is significant to the wise leader."*

This chapter details all of the major screens in the game and the parts and options of each. Refer to the body of the manual for the whys and wherefores (all we're discussing here is the how-to). The screens are covered in the order you're most likely to encounter them, for ease of reference.

## The Main Menu

This menu is what you see when you first start the *Civilization III* program.

**New Game:** Begin an entirely new game. Choosing this option means going through the pre-game options screens, which we explain below.

**Quick Start:** Start a new game using the same game settings as the last New Game played.

**Tutorial:** Starts a new game, with a random civilization, on the easiest difficulty. It also displays helpful Tutorial information to ease new players into the game.

**Load Game:** Load and continue a previously saved game. A dialog box lists all of the saved games available. Choose the game you wish to load.

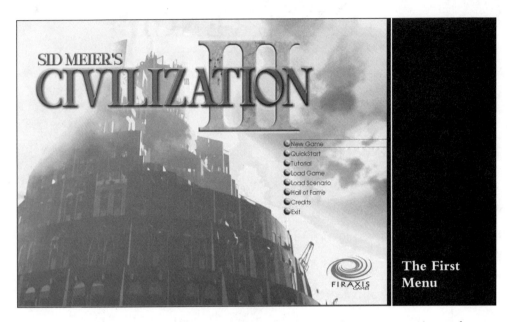

The First
Menu

**Load Scenario:** Load a scenario. You can create your own game scenarios or play scenarios your friends have constructed to challenge you. To load successfully, scenarios *must* have been created with the *Civilization III* CD-ROM game. Older scenarios from other *Civilization* games are not compatible.

**Hall of Fame:** See the standings attained by the most successful rulers in previous games.

**Preferences:** Sets your in-game preferences.

**Audio Preferences:** Adjusts the volume settings for the game.

**Credits:** Find out who's responsible for creating the game.

**Exit:** Quit the game.

Double-click the option of your choice.

## World Setup Screen

When you start a new game, this screen gives you control over all the important aspects of the planet for which you'll be contending.

When you are happy with all your choices, click the O icon to continue to the Player Setup screen. To return to the Main menu, select the X icon.

**Land Mass and Water Coverage**

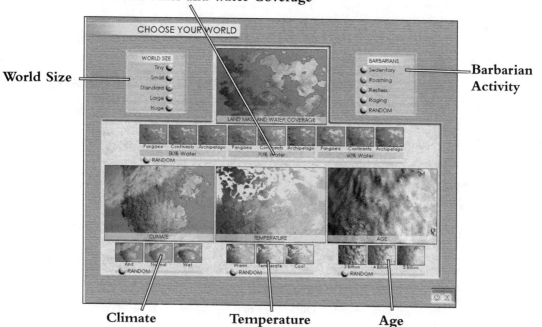

World Size

Barbarian Activity

Climate       Temperature       Age

## World Size

By choosing the size of the map, you determine how much territory there is and, to a large degree, how long the game takes to play.

**Tiny:** This size map leads to short, intensely contested games. Tribes find each other quickly.

**Small:** These games are slightly less intense than those on tiny maps. You'll still run into your opponents quickly.

**Standard:** This is the standard size map.

**Large:** This sprawling map takes longer to explore and exploit. Consequently, games go on longer.

**Huge:** Games played on this size map allow plenty of development time before tribes meet one another. Wars tend to be prolonged and tough. You'll have to work hard to dominate this size world before you run out of game time.

## Land Mass and Water Coverage

This option sets the percentage of terrain squares that are water versus land, as well as the form of that land. There are three Water Coverage settings, each with three Land Mass settings.

**80% Ocean:** Choosing this option gives your world a small number of land squares and a larger number of ocean squares.

**70% Ocean:** This option yields land and ocean squares roughly equivalent to that of our own Earth.

**60% Ocean:** This option produces a larger number of land squares and a small number of ocean squares.

These parameters determine how your world's land is shaped into land masses, taking the ocean coverage setting into account.

**Archipelago:** This option produces large numbers of relatively small continents.

**Continents:** This option yields a few large land masses and a few smaller ones.

**Pangaea:** Choosing this gives you one large supercontinent.

**Random:** This option chooses Water Coverage and Land Mass settings at random.

## Climate

The Climate parameter sets the relative frequency with which particular terrain types—especially Desert and Jungle—occur.

**Arid:** Choosing this option gives your world a larger number of dry terrain squares, such as Plains and Desert.

**Normal:** This option yields about equal numbers of wet and dry terrain squares.

**Wet:** This option produces a larger number of wet terrain squares, such as Jungle and Flood Plain.

**Random:** Use this to have a Climate setting selected at random.

# Age

This parameter determines how long erosion, continental drift, and tectonic activity have had to sculpt your world.

**3 Billion Years:** This option yields a young, rough world, in which terrain types occur in clusters.

**4 Billion Years:** This option yields a middle-aged world, one in which plate tectonics have been acting to diversify terrain.

**5 Billion Years:** This option produces an old world, one in which the tectonics have settled down somewhat, allowing erosion and other natural forces to soften the terrain features.

**Random:** This option selects a random Age setting.

# Temperature

This parameter determines the relative frequency with which particular terrain types occur.

**Cool:** This option produces larger numbers of cold and cool terrain squares, such as Tundra.

**Temperate:** Choosing this option gives your world an average number of each terrain type.

**Warm:** This option yields a larger number of tropical terrains, like Desert and Jungle.

**Random:** This option chooses a Temperature setting at random.

# Barbarian

You can also set the level of barbarian activity in the game.

**Villages:** Players who really hate barbarians can choose to play in this ideal world. Barbarians are restricted to their encampments. The surrounding terrain is free of their mischief.

**Roaming:** Barbarian settlements occasionally appear, but less frequently and in smaller numbers than at higher levels. This is the standard level of barbarian activity.

**Restless:** Barbarians appear in moderate up to significant numbers, at shorter intervals than at lower levels.

**Raging:** You asked for it! The world is full of barbarians, and they appear in large numbers.

**Random:** This option selects a random Barbarian setting.

## Player Setup Screen

The Player Setup screen is where you decide who you'll be and how tough a challenge you're ready for. You can also customize the way the game works. In the center is your Leader Portrait, a preview of how you'll appear to other civilizations in the game.

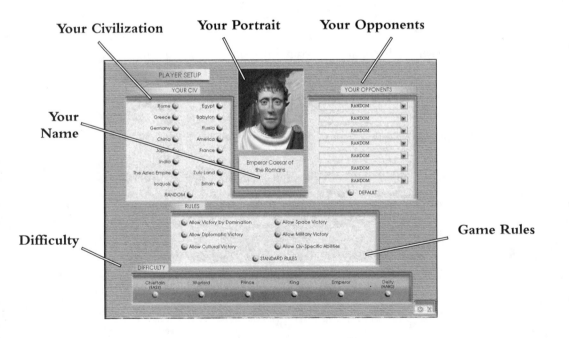

When you are happy with all your choices, click the O icon to begin the game. To return to the World Setup screen, select the X icon.

## Your Opponents

Along the top of this screen are slots for the other civilizations that will be in the game. Using these, you can control how many competitors you face and—within limits—who they are. You can set each slot to one of three states:

- **None** means that no civilization is in that slot. If you want to play against fewer than the maximum number of competitors, close a few slots.

- A **Filled** slot contains the name of a specific civilization that you've selected. This guarantees that the tribe you chose will be in the game when it starts.

- **Random** is the option to use when you don't want to close the slot, but you don't want to choose a specific civilization either. The game will choose an opponent for you.

## Your Civilization

Select the tribe you want to rule from the options available. Every tribe has different strengths, weaknesses, and one special unit, as listed in the following chart.

| Civilization | Qualities* | Starting Advances | Special Unit | Replaces |
|---|---|---|---|---|
| Rome | Industrious, Militaristic | Masonry, Warrior Code | Legionary | Swordsman |
| Greece | Scientific, Commercial | Bronze Working, Alphabet | Hoplite | Spearman |
| Germany | Militaristic, Scientific | Warrior Code, Bronze Working | Panzer | Tank |
| China | Industrious, Scientific | Masonry, Bronze Working | Rider | Knight |
| Japan | Militaristic, Religious | Warrior Code, Ceremonial Burial | Samurai | Knight |
| India | Religious, Commercial | Ceremonial Burial, Alphabet | War Elephant | Knight |
| Aztecs | Militaristic, Religious | Warrior Code, Ceremonial Burial | Jaguar Warrior | Warrior |
| Iroquois | Expansionist, Religious | Pottery, Ceremonial Burial | Mounted Warrior | Horseman |
| Egypt | Industrious, Religious | Masonry, Ceremonial Burial | War Chariot | Chariot |
| Babylon | Religious, Scientific | Ceremonial Burial, Bronze Working | Bowman | Archer |
| Russia | Expansionist, Scientific | Pottery, Bronze Working | Cossack | Cavalry |

| Civilization | Qualities* | Starting Advances | Special Unit | Replaces |
|---|---|---|---|---|
| America | Industrious, Expansionist | Masonry, Pottery | F-15 | Jet Fighter |
| France | Industrious, Commercial | Masonry, Alphabet | Musketeer | Musket Man |
| Persia | Militaristic, Commercial | Warrior Code, Alphabet | Immortals | Swordsman |
| Zulus | Militaristic, Expansionist | Pottery, Warrior Code | Impi | Warrior |
| Britain | Expansionist, Commercial | Pottery, Alphabet | Man-o-War | Frigate |

*The civilization qualities describe both the general character of the tribe and its advantages.

**Commercial:** Cities with large populations produce extra commerce. Levels of corruption are lower.

**Expansionist:** Begin the game with a Scout. Barbarian villages are more lucrative.

**Industrious:** Workers complete jobs faster. Cities with large populations produce extra shields.

**Militaristic:** Military city improvements (like Barracks and Coastal Fortresses) are cheaper. Unit promotions (to regular, veteran, and elite) occur more frequently.

**Religious:** Religious city improvements (like Temples and Cathedrals) are cheaper. Anarchy lasts only one turn during revolutions.

**Scientific:** Scientific city improvements (like Libraries and Universities) are cheaper. Gain a bonus civilization advance at the start of each new era.

If you'd like to rename yourself, just select the default leader name for your chosen civilization and type in your new name.

## Difficulty Levels

Choose the level of difficulty at which you wish to play. A number of factors are adjusted at each difficulty level, including the general level of discontent among your citizens and the average craftiness and intelligence of the AI leaders.

**Chieftain:** This easiest level is recommended for first-time players.

**Warlord:** Warlord level best suits the occasional player who doesn't want too difficult a test.

**Prince:** At this difficulty level, everything comes much less easily, and your rivals are significantly better at managing their empires. You need some experience and skill to win.

**Monarch:** Experienced and skilled players often play at this level, where the crafty enemy leaders and the unstable attitude of your citizens combine to present a significant challenge.

**Emperor:** This level is for those who feel the need to be humbled. Your opponents will no longer pull their punches; if you want to win, you'll have to earn it.

**Deity:** This is the ultimate *Civilization* challenge, for those who think they've learned to beat the game. You'll have to give a virtuoso performance to survive at this level (and yes, it is possible—theoretically—to win on Deity level). Good luck!

## Game Rules

Tweaking the parameters of the game can change the whole flavor of the challenge. The custom rules offer several different possibilities. You can reset to the default standards by clicking Restore Default Rules.

**Allow Victory by Domination:** If this box is checked, players can win by conquering and controlling two-thirds of the world's territory. The other civilizations, or what's left of them, capitulate to your rule.

**Allow Diplomatic Victory:** Unless this option is unchecked, leaders can win by purely diplomatic means. To be successful, a ruler must be elected Secretary-General through a vote of the United Nations.

**Allow Cultural Victory:** Make sure this option is checked, and any civilization can win the game through overwhelming cultural dominance. For success, a nation must have accumulated enough cultural points.

**Allow Space Victory:** When this box is checked, players can build spaceship parts and win the game by being the first to launch a spaceship bound for Alpha Centauri.

**Allow Military Victory:** If this box is checked, players can win by eliminating all rival nations. If you're the last one standing, you rule the world.

**Allow Civ-Specific Abilities:** This option controls the diversity factor. When it's checked, each civilization has its own unique strengths and weaknesses (as listed earlier in this section). Turning this off is handy for leveling the playing field.

# Map Screen

The Map screen is the isometric map, the window in which you view and move your active units. The area shown in this window is the section of the world outlined in the World Map.

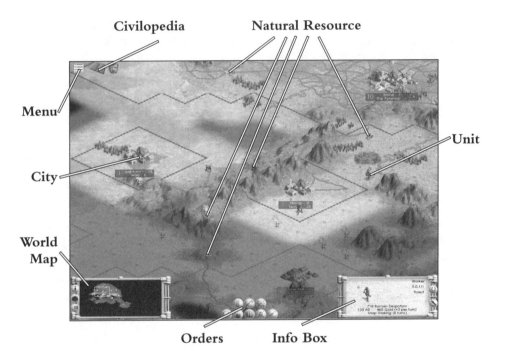

## Zooming the View

You can switch the scale of the main map view between two options using the Zoom shortcut key [Z]. Zoom out to see more territory, then zoom back in to see more detail.

## Moving the View

To reposition the Map screen so that it shows a different section of the game map, simply click anywhere in the window. The map is redrawn to center on the square you clicked. If you want to center on a square that is not presently in the main Map screen, click on a location in the World Map.

If the area you want to see isn't far off the screen, or if you want to scan the territory between your current view and the destination, you can scroll the map. Just move your mouse cursor to any edge of the Map screen; the view moves to show you the territory in that direction. When you move the cursor away from the edge (or if you reach one of the poles), the scrolling stops. You can also use the arrow keys (*not* the arrows on the numeric keypad) to move your view.

## Centering on the Active Unit

To center the view on the active unit, press [C] or click on the picture of the unit in the Info Box. This is especially useful when the active unit is out of sight off the screen or partially hidden behind the Status or World Map.

## Giving a Unit Orders

Near the bottom of the Map screen is a group of circular buttons. These are the *orders*, which you use to control the active unit. Read "Orders," a little later in this chapter, for descriptions of the various orders.

## Looking into a City

To get a look inside one of your cities, double-click on the city. You can also right-click on the city and select Zoom to {City Name} from the mini-menu. This opens the City Display for that burg. Read "City Display," later in this chapter, for the detailed description of that screen.

## Changing a City's Production

To change the current project a city is working on, press the [Shift] key and right-click on the city while in the Map screen. Then choose a new project from the menu that opens.

## Renaming a City

To rename one of your cities, right-click on the city, then select Rename {City Name}.

## The Buttons

Near the top left corner of the Map screen is a small group of icons. Clicking these activates one of three very useful features: the game menus, the Civilopedia, or your advisors. Read "Menus," "Advisors," or "Civilopedia," later in this chapter, for more details.

## Using an Embassy or Spy

If you've built an embassy with another civilization or planted a spy, an icon at that nation's capital city notes that. To give orders to that embassy or spy, double-click the embassy icon or spy icon. For more information, please see **Chapter 13: Diplomacy and Trade**.

# World Map

This little mini-map, in the lower left corner of the screen, shows an overview of the entire known world. The rectangle on this map delineates the edges of the Map screen view.

You can use the World Map to move rapidly around the Map screen. Click on a location in the World Map, and the Map window shifts to center on that position.

A handy button on the edge of this box toggles between two World Map modes.

You can toggle the World Map on and off (along with everything else except the Map itself) by pressing [Del].

# Info Box

The Info Box is dedicated to information on the current active unit and on the status of your civilization and your game. There are two buttons on the edge of this box:

 **Initiate Diplomacy** requests a dialogue with a selected rival leader. You can only use this to contact those leaders with whom you already have communications.

 Click on **Initiate Espionage** when you have espionage options available to establish embassies and plant spies.

The following information is included in the Info Box, not necessarily in this order:

- **Unit icon:** The active unit is represented by its icon. This icon includes the nationality color and the bar noting damage status.

- **Move indicator:** This tracks how much of its movement allowance the unit has left in this turn. Green means a full allowance remains; yellow means the unit has moved, but it still has some allowance left; red means that the unit has used up its entire allowance.

- **Nationality:** The unit's nationality (if it's different from that of its owner) is listed just before the unit's type.

- **Type:** This is the name of the type of unit—*Catapult*, for example.

- **Rank:** If the unit is a military unit, the Info Box tells you its experience level—conscript, regular, veteran, or elite.

- **A/D/M rating:** The unit's attack, defense, and movement ratings are listed, along with the number of movement points remaining to the unit. Also remember that units beginning on a square containing a railroad and moving along the railroad spend no movement points until they leave the railroad.

- **Terrain:** This lists the terrain type of the square in which the unit is located.

- **Government:** Below the unit icon, the Info Box lists your civilization's name and current form of government.

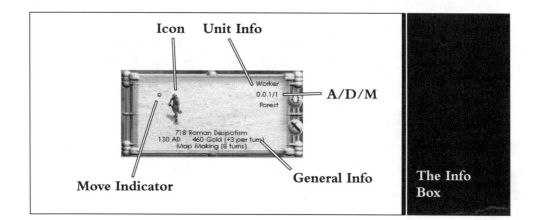

- **Date:** The date is reported in years BC or AD. A normal game begins in 4000 BC. Each turn represents the passing of a period of years. Depending on the current date, turns might be 20, 25, 40, or 50 years long.

- **Treasury:** This figure reports the amount of gold currently in your treasury and the rate of change per turn. If it's increasing, you've got a surplus; if it's decreasing, you're operating at a deficit.

- **Scientific research:** The research indicator notes your current research goal and how many turns are remaining before its discovery is completed.

# Orders

Which options are in the rows of Orders icons at the bottom of the Map screen depends on the abilities of the active unit and its situation. Orders that are inappropriate or not currently available for the active unit simply don't appear.

## Airlift ([T])

Use this order to move a unit that has not yet moved this turn from any of your cities served by an Airport to any of your other cities with an Airport. This travel uses all of the unit's movement points for that turn. Only one unit can be airlifted from or into each city per turn.

## Automate Worker ([A])

If you would rather not give a Worker specific commands every time it finishes a job, you can automate it. Automated Workers will not add themselves to cities, but will work to improve terrain around existing ones. In some situations, control of the Worker reverts to you.

## Bombard ([B])

Use this to order a unit capable of bombardment to use that ability to damage any suitable target within range.

## Build Army ([B])

Use this to order a leader to create an Army. For more information about Armies, please read **Chapter 8: Units**.

## Build Colony ([B])

Use this to order a Worker to build a colony in the square it occupies. Colonies collect strategic resources and luxuries from squares outside your borders and transfer them via road to the city. Enemy units can't take over an undefended colony, but can easily destroy it.

## Build Fortress ([Ctrl]-[F])

This orders a Worker to build defensive fortifications in the square it occupies. Once it is built, your units can occupy the Fortress to enhance their defensive capabilities. This order is not available until you have discovered Construction.

## Build Irrigation ([I])

Use this order to have a Worker irrigate the square in which it stands.

## Build Mine ([M])

Use this order to make a Worker mine the square in which it stands.

## Build Railroad ([R])

If you have discovered Steam Power, you can order your Workers to upgrade existing roads by laying track for railroads.

## Build Road ([R])

This order tells a Worker to build roads across the square in which it stands.

## Build/Join City ([B])

This tells a Settler to create a new town where it stands. Note that you cannot build cities in terrain squares directly adjacent to an existing city. You also cannot build on Mountains.

If a Settler or Worker stands in an existing city, this orders that unit to add itself to the city. Workers add one and Settlers add two population points.

## Clean Up Pollution ([Shift]-[C])

Use this order to tell a Worker to detoxify a polluted square.

## Clear or Replant Forest ([N] or [Shift]-[C])

Click this order to have a Worker clear the Forest square in which it stands or reforest a square that's devoid of trees. This results in a change in the square's terrain type, generally for the better. Clearing a Forest also provides a few shields for the nearest friendly city. If your unit stands in a square that can't be cleared or reforested, the order doesn't appear.

## Clear Jungle ([Shift]-[C])

Click this order to have a Worker clear the Jungle square in which it stands. This results in a change in the square's terrain type, generally for the better. If your unit stands in a square that can't be cleared, the order doesn't appear.

## Disband ([D])

This order allows you to dismiss a unit from active duty. The unit disappears completely and irrevocably, so be careful when invoking this option. If you disband a unit in a city square, a fraction of the unit's construction cost is immediately added to the Production Box in that city. This represents the redistribution of support and materials and retraining of soldiers.

## Fortify/Garrison ([F])

Select this order to have a military unit dig in and fortify itself in the square in which it stands or garrison itself in a city. This enhances the defensive capabilities of the unit for as long as it remains fortified—which is until you activate it. The exception is a damaged unit, which will reactivate itself when it reaches full strength. You can "fortify" defenseless units (such as Settlers and Workers) to have them stay in one place, but they gain no defensive benefit.

## GoTo ([G])

This order allows you to send a unit directly to a selected square. After you click the order, move your mouse cursor to the destination. The number of turns it will take to reach the highlighted square is shown. Click on a square, and the unit will go there without further orders.

## Airdrop ([A])

This movement order is available only to airdrop-capable units (i.e., Paratroopers and Helicopters) that are currently located in a city with an Airport. Choose any unoccupied square within range of the unit's current location. The unit will move immediately to that square. This order uses all of the unit's movement points for that turn.

## Pillage ([P])

This order tells a military unit to wreak havoc on the square it occupies, destroying terrain improvements. That can mean collapsing a mine, destroying irrigation, ripping up roads, or other destruction.

## Hold (Spacebar)

Use this order to pass over a unit for a turn and have it hold its current position. The unit takes no action, but will repair itself somewhat if it has been damaged.

## Load/Unload ([L])

Give this order to a ship to activate all its passenger units, allowing them to move ashore or onto another ship. The ship must be adjacent to a land square, a city square, or another friendly ship. You can also click on the ship to bring up a box showing all the shipboard units.

## Wait ([W] or [Tab])

Use this to order the current active unit to wait for orders until you have given every other active unit something to do. Note that if you give another unit the Wait order, that unit will get in line behind the first unit you ordered to wait, and so forth.

## Air Missions

All of the possible missions that air units can carry out have their own orders buttons.

**Bombing mission ([B]):** Drop bombs on the selected terrain square or enemy city. Air bombardment affects city improvements and city populations.

**Recon mission ([R]):** Investigate the selected square and its surrounding squares.

**Re-base Mission ([Shift]-[R]):** Relocate the unit's base of operations to another city or an aircraft carrier.

**Air superiority mission ([S]):** Scout the unit's defensive range (half of its operational range). This is similar to the Fortify order in that it remains the unit's assignment until you reactivate the unit in order to give it other orders. Only fighters (including the F-15) are capable of flying air superiority missions.

**Airdrop mission:** Carry a single ground unit to a specified location, land, and drop the unit off, leaving it there. Only Helicopters can airdrop ground units, and then only within their operational range. This "vertical insertion" cannot place a unit into a square that contains an enemy unit.

# Menus

Click the Menu icon on the Map screen, and the Main menu opens. The options on this menu open other menus, as follows.

## Game Menu

The Game menu is where you save, load, and quit, among other handy and indispensable features.

**Load Game:** This is the one you use to load a previously saved game and continue playing. Choose from the saved games listed.

**New Game:** To end your current game (without saving) and start fresh, use this option.

**Preferences:** Use this to customize the way the game functions.

**Quit:** Leave your current game immediately, without saving.

**Resign:** End the current game, but compute and display your final score and the wrap-up screens.

**Save Game:** Use this to save your current game (to continue playing later).

## Info Screens Menu

The Info Screens let you check on your progress.

**Histograph:** The Histograph tracks and displays the balance of power in the world throughout history. You can select comparisons based on culture, power, or Civilization Score. You can choose a scale for the vertical axis based on turns or years. On the right is a score comparison of all the tribes in the game and a detailed breakdown of your own score.

**Palace:** As you rule, your citizens will sometimes offer to improve your imperial palace. In between those times, you can view your estate using this option.

**Spaceship:** When you have started work on your ship to Alpha Centauri, use this option to take a look at your progress.

**Demographics:** This provides an interesting overview of the citizens of your empire.

## Map Menu

The Map menu contains some features you'll find useful when you're looking over your world.

**Grid:** Toggles the map grid markings on and off.

**Center Screen:** Redraws the map view so that the current active unit is in the center of your observation area.

**Clean Map:** Toggles the display of man-made objects on the map. These include cities, units, and terrain improvements.

**Locate City:** This is the quickest way to find a city. Choose from the list, and the map view is redrawn to center on the city you select.

**Zoom Out/In:** Use this to enlarge or diminish the scope of your map view.

# City Display

You can direct the operation of any of your cities from the City Display. Here, you assign citizens to work in the surrounding fields, mines, forests, and fishing grounds. This display collects in one place all critical information concerning the pictured city's status: how many shields it produces, how much food and commerce it is generating, what it is producing and how close the item is to completion, the happiness of the population, who's defending the city, what improvements you've already built, and more.

You can open the City Display in a couple of ways:

- Position your mouse cursor over a city in the Map screen, then double-click on that city.

- Click on a city name in any Advisor's report.

- Right-click on any city on the Map screen, then select Zoom to {City} from the mini-menu.

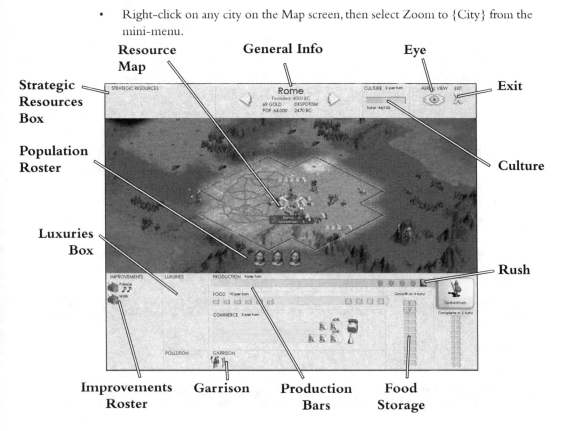

Resource Map

General Info

Eye

Strategic Resources Box

Exit

Population Roster

Culture

Luxuries Box

Rush

Improvements Roster

Garrison

Production Bars

Food Storage

You can close the City Display by clicking the Exit button or pressing [Esc].

## General Info

Near the top of the display is some useful information: the name of the city, the year in which it was founded, and its total population.

- The two arrow buttons allow you to scroll through all the cities in your empire.

- Clicking the Eye takes you to the Aerial View, for a panoramic look at your city in all its glory.

- The Exit button closes the City Display.

## Resource Map

The bulk of the City Display is a detail map showing the explored terrain squares around the city. The squares within the City Radius are highlighted, and each worked square is marked with the resources being derived from it. The city square itself is always under production. For each citizen, you can work one additional square. The maximum number of squares a city can work is the number of citizens plus one or 21, whichever is smaller. Note that it is possible to have more citizens than there are squares to work.

Depending on the type of terrain in a map square, citizens working there can produce food, production (shields), and commerce. Most squares produce a combination of several resources. Clicking on any square under production (except the city square, which remains permanently under production) temporarily takes that citizen off work. Click on an unoccupied square to put the citizen back to work in a new place. Simply by clicking the selected squares, you can move citizens from one square to another to change the mix of resources the city is harvesting. Citizens removed from work are temporarily converted into Entertainers.

### A Convenient Shortcut

To have the city governors assign the city's citizens to work according to the priorities you have given them, click the city square. See "City Governors" below for more information.

When a city's population increases, each citizen is automatically assigned an area to develop. You might want to review the map of a city that has just increased in size to be certain that laborers have been placed as you wish.

## Population Roster

This is a roster of citizen icons representing the city's population. Each icon in the Population Roster represents one population "point." Citizens can be happy, content, unhappy, or resisting. If the number of unhappy people exceeds the number of happy people (content people, resistors, and Specialists are ignored), that city goes into civil disorder (see "Civil Disorder" in **Chapter 11: Managing Your Cities** for details). In addition to the usual folks, a city can support three different types of Specialists.

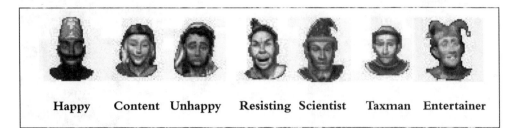

| Happy | Content | Unhappy | Resisting | Scientist | Taxman | Entertainer |

Citizens who are not working and producing within the City Radius are *Specialists*. (The exception is resistors, who refuse to work.) For an example, click on a productive City Radius square; the laborers there become Entertainers (one citizen in the Population Roster is replaced by an Entertainer). Specialists no longer directly contribute to the resources a city generates, but they do consume food like other citizens. However, they can be useful in adjusting the happiness of the population and the amounts of taxes and research the city generates. There are three types of Specialists: Entertainers, Scientists, and Taxmen.

**Entertainers:** Citizens removed from the work force immediately become Entertainers. Each Entertainer generates one happy face, making one unhappy citizen content or (if there are no unhappy ones) one content citizen happy.

**Taxmen:** Click on an Entertainer in the Population Roster to put him to work as a Taxman. Each Taxman produces one gold.

**Scientists:** Click on a Taxman to create a Scientist. Each Scientist adds one to the raw science production (instead of the income the Taxman used to generate). Click on a Scientist icon to return it to Entertainer status.

**Resistors:** These are the citizens in a captured city who resent your rule and refuse to work.

## The City Production Bars

The Production bars compile all the resources generated by the city's laborers each turn. Food, shields, and commerce income are collected each turn from the City Radius squares being worked by citizens. The amount of any particular resource collected might be modified by the presence of a certain improvement in the city, the form of government you choose, or by your ownership of a certain Wonder.

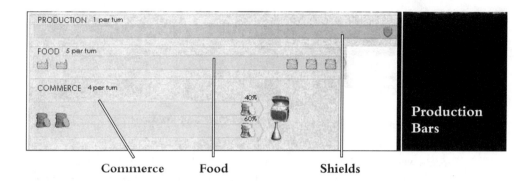

Commerce     Food     Shields

**Production bar:** The "shields" bar represents the state of the city's production each turn. Depending on the form of government under which your civilization operates and a few other factors, some of the shields generated each turn might be lost to waste (red shields); this is also noted. Production over and above waste (blue shields) accumulates toward what the city is building in the Production Box.

**Food bar:** The food bar represents the state of the city's harvest each turn. Every citizen in your city consumes two units of food each turn. Any surplus or shortfall is noted. Excess accumulates in the Food Storage Box.

**Commerce bars:** These bars measure the city's income from commerce and how it's apportioned. One bar notes what portion of the city's income is being sent to your empire's treasury. Another notes what portion is going to fund research. The last lists how much is being sent to entertainment. These numbers depend on your science and entertainment rates. Depending on your type of government, the number of cities in your civilization, and each city's distance from your capital, some portion of the overall commerce might be lost to corruption (which is also noted on the bars). The apportionment is figured after the losses to corruption have been subtracted.

## The Luxuries Box

The Luxuries Box shows what types of luxuries are affecting this city's citizens. The box shows all of the luxury resources the city is connected to. These have a direct and powerful effect on your population's happiness. Only one of each type has a happiness effect, so only one of each is ever displayed. The number of "happy faces" displayed after each luxury resource indicates the number of citizens affected by it.

# Food Storage Box

Any surplus food generated by your city each turn accumulates in this box. The capacity of the box expands as the city's population increases. When the box overflows, your

city's population grows by one point, and a new citizen is added to the Population Roster. The Food Storage Box empties and begins to fill again the next turn. A note at the top of the box tells you how long it will be at the current rate of accumulation before the city produces its next citizen.

If the city is not producing enough food to feed its population, the shortage is subtracted from the reserve in the Food Storage Box. If the box is empty and the city still has a food shortfall, the city loses one point of population each turn due to starvation, until equilibrium is reached.

The Granary improvement has the effect of speeding population growth. When a city has a Granary, the Food Storage Box only half empties when it overflows and creates more people. The box empties only to the granary line. The Pyramids Wonder has the same effect, but for all cities on the same continent rather than just one.

# Production Box

Next to your Food Storage Box is the Production Box. The net production generated by your city each turn accumulates here. The capacity of the Production Box changes to reflect the cost of the unit, improvement, or Wonder currently under construction. When the box is full, the item is complete. The box empties, and the new item is ready for use.

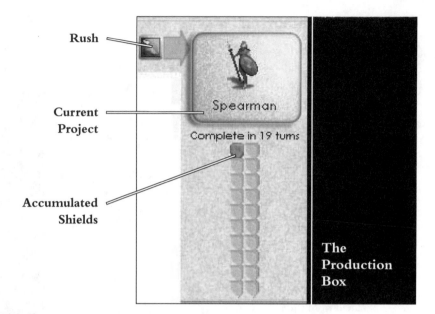

Rush

Current
Project

Accumulated
Shields

The
Production
Box

The item being built is noted at the top. The items available for building depend on the advances your civilization has achieved. To change the current project, click on the icon and select from the list that opens. If you have already accumulated sufficient shields to construct the new choice, any excess is lost, and the item is completed in the next turn. Otherwise, the accumulated shields roll over toward the new item.

When the discovery of a new advance makes available a unit that supersedes units currently being built, your production is automatically upgraded to the new unit. If you are building a Wonder and another civilization completes it before you can, your city will automatically switch to the most costly project available.

You can speed the completion of an item by clicking the Rush button. A dialog box shows the price the rush job requires you to pay. (See "Rush Jobs" in **Chapter 11: Managing Your Cities** for why you might choose this option.)

You can queue up production choices by holding down the [Shift] key and clicking on the item in the production list. Once the current production is complete, the city governors will select the next item in the queue.

## Improvement Roster

The Improvement Roster is a list of all of the existing improvements and Wonders of the World in the city. Each entry in the list includes the item's icon and name. If the improvement is one that requires a maintenance payment each turn, there is an icon noting this next to the listing. An icon denotes any improvement that has a cultural effect, as well. Finally, those improvements that affect citizens' happiness have "happy faces" as a measure of their effect.

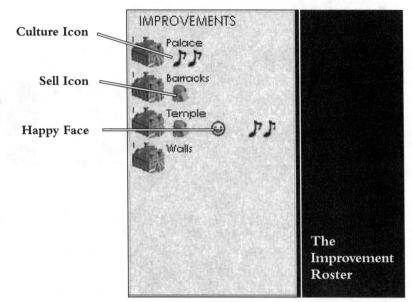

**Culture Icon**

**Sell Icon**

**Happy Face**

The Improvement Roster

Improvements are added to the roster as they are completed. Right-click on any listing to sell it. (You have a chance to cancel before the sale becomes final.) You cannot sell Wonders. Any improvements destroyed by disaster or bombardment are removed from the list, as are any improvements you sell. Note that Wonders will remain on the roster even after their special ability has become obsolete.

## Empire Info Box

The Empire Info Box contains some handy bits of data, including:

*   Your current form of government

- The date
- The amount of gold in your treasury

This box also keeps track of the city's culture points. The number this city is earning per turn is noted, then the total accumulated and the amount needed for the next expansion of the city's sphere of influence. The bar below that gives you a graphic representation of your progress toward this goal.

## Garrison

The Garrison displays all of the units currently in the city. The health status of each unit is indicated on its bar. Right-click on any unit icon to open the Orders mini-menu for

that unit. The orders you can give using this menu are exactly like those you would give the active unit, except that only those orders appropriate to a unit inside a city are available.

## Pollution Box

The threat of pollution as a result of the industrial production and smog in the city is noted on the City Display—represented by cautionary icons. The more of these that appear, the greater the likelihood that a random terrain square within the City Radius will become polluted this turn.

# City Governors

When a city completes a building project, it selects another one. The city *governors* do this. Unless you give specific instructions, the governors will choose what to produce next by guessing at what you want. These guesses are based on the history of production orders you've given throughout the game. You can give your governors specific guidelines to follow in their selection of projects. At the City Display, press [G] to open the City Governors window.

By selecting options in each column, you give instructions that cover only the current city, all your cities, or only those cities on the same continent as the current one. On the General governor page, options are:

- **Manage citizens:** This gives the governors your permission to control the allocation of citizen laborers to the terrain in the City Radius. Using the next three options, you instruct them as to your priorities for this task. If you select more than one of these three, the governors strike a balance between those you've chosen.

    - **Emphasize food** – instructs the governors to maximize the food produced.

    - **Emphasize shields** – instructs the governors to maximize shield production.

    - **Emphasize commerce** – instructs the governors to maximize commerce.

- **Manage production:** This gives the governors your permission to assign building projects as they see fit. Using the next two options, you can put limits on what they're allowed to do.

    - **Never start Wonders** – tells the governors not to begin construction of a Wonder.

    - **Never start Small Wonders** – tells the governors not to begin construction of a Small Wonder.

Click the Production button to switch to the Production governor page. Here, you can give your governors some more detailed production orders. Specifically, for every one of the options, you can specify how often the governor should select to produce that particular thing. This effectively provides your governors with a list of priorities. You can set priorities for:

- **Offensive ground units** – those units that are stronger on offense than defense

- **Defensive ground units** – those units that are stronger on defense than offense

- **Artillery** – strictly offensive bombardment units, like Catapults

- **Settlers** – Settlers

- **Workers** – Workers

- **Naval units** – seagoing vessels

- **Air units** – flying units

- **Growth** – city improvements that increase the rate of population growth in the city

- **Production** – city improvements that improve the shield production in the city

- **Happiness** – city improvements that add to the happiness of your citizens

- **Science** – city improvements that boost the scientific research output of the city
- **Wealth** – city improvements that increase the tax income the city produces
- **Trade** – city improvements that augment the city's commerce production
- **Exploration** – units whose primary role is exploration, like Scouts and Explorers
- **Culture** – city improvements that build the city's cultural influence

# Advisors

Click on the Advisors icon on the Map screen to consult with your advisors. These useful folks provide reports on the overall picture of your civilization's strengths and progress.

## Domestic Advisor

This advisor summarizes the internal state of your empire, including your overall income, how it's being used, and the status of all your cities. You can open this screen from the Game menu or by pressing [F1].

**Advice:** Every advisor offers advice on an ongoing basis. You might find it useful, so pay attention.

**Income box:** This lists what's currently in your treasury and your empire's total income per turn, from all sources. It also lists your per-turn expenses in detail, then does the arithmetic and displays the net gain (or loss) your treasury experiences every turn.

**Science ratio:** Use this slider to control what percentage (in 10% increments) of your per-turn income is allocated to scientific research. Click at either end of the bar to move the slider in that direction.

**Entertainment spending:** This slider controls how much of your per-turn income is dedicated to providing entertainment to keep your citizens happy. Click at either end of the bar to move the slider in that direction. The number of "happy faces" the current setting generates is noted.

**Info boxes:** These two little boxes note your current type of government and mobilization status (normal or mobilized for war). Click on either to make a change.

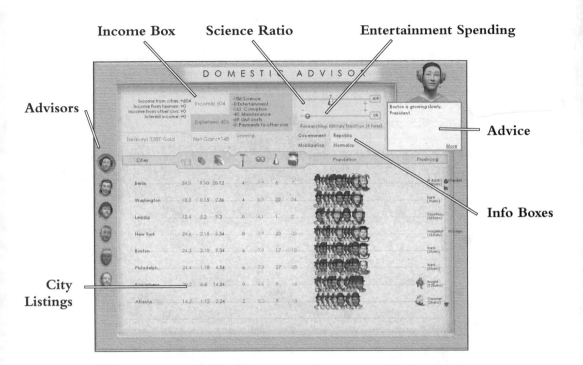

**Income Box**    **Science Ratio**    **Entertainment Spending**

**Advisors**

**Advice**

**Info Boxes**

**City Listings**

**City listings:** This report lists the vital statistics for all the cities in your empire, in the order in which they were founded. This information includes how many of each resource type (food, production, and commerce) each is collecting, the size of each city, and the Population Roster (happy, content, etc. citizens). Cities in civil disorder are marked. It lists what each city is building and how close it is to finishing that assignment. The maintenance cost paid by the city each turn is tracked, as is the city's contribution to the treasury and scientific research. Finally, the number of "happy faces" generated in the city is listed. You can double-click on any of the listed names to open the City Display for that city.

**Advisors:** As on every advisor's screen, the icons for the other advisors appear to one side. Click on any one to go to that advisor's report.

# Trade Advisor

Your Trade Advisor reports on the state of your trade network, your trade agreements with other civilizations, and what you have available to offer in trade. You can open this screen from the Game menu or by hitting [F2].

**Existing Trades**  **Networked Cities**

**Advisors**

**Advice**

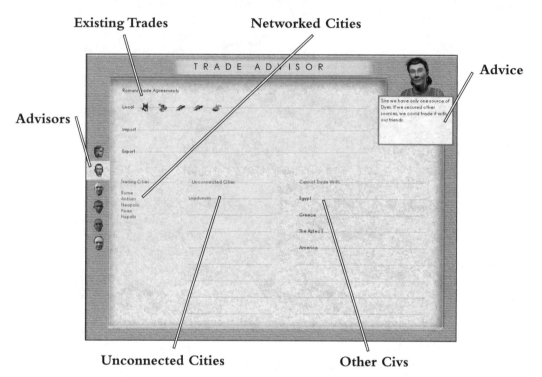

**Unconnected Cities**  **Other Civs**

**Advice:** Every advisor offers advice on an ongoing basis. You might find it useful, so pay attention.

**Trade agreements:** This box lists all of the strategic resources and luxuries that are being shared throughout your internal trade network. Below that are all of the ongoing trade agreements you have with other civilizations.

**Networked cities:** This list contains all of the cities in your empire that are connected to your trade network and enjoying the benefits thereof.

**Unconnected cities:** On this list are the cities not connected to your trade network. You really should work on shortening this.

**Other civs:** Any other civilizations you've made contact with are tracked in this box, including notations on what resources each has available for trade, which nations you have a trade network connection to, and which you don't. Click on any listing to contact that leader.

**Advisors:** As on every advisor's screen, the icons for the other advisors appear to one side. Click on any one to go to that advisor's report.

## Military Advisor

The Military Advisor reports on your military assets and those of your rivals. This includes information on every one of your existing units, whether in cities or out in

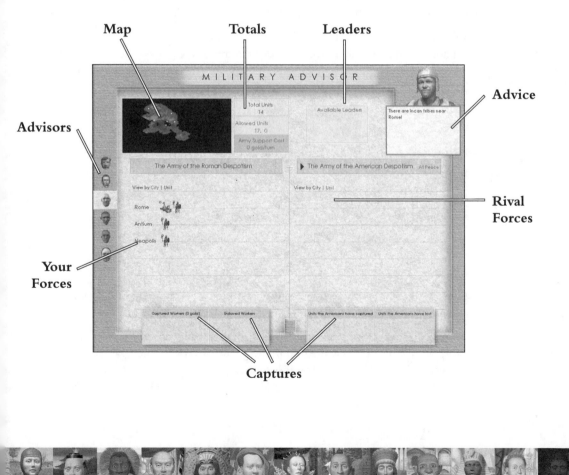

the world, plus captured units. You can open this screen from the Game menu or by pressing [F3].

**Advice:** Every advisor offers advice on an ongoing basis. You might find it useful, so pay attention.

**Map:** It can be helpful to refer to the strategic map when planning an upcoming or ongoing campaign.

**Totals:** These boxes list the total number of units you control, the number of units you can support for free, and the amount you're paying every turn to support your military forces.

**Leaders:** If any leaders have joined your nation's forces but have not yet been used to create an Army or speed up a Wonder, they're listed here.

**Your forces:** All of your units and their current hit point status appear in this listing. The two text buttons allow you to group the listed units either by city or type of unit.

**Rival forces:** Those units of a selected rival that your advisor knows about and whatever information he has about them are listed in this box. Use the selection bar at the top to choose which nation's forces you want to view. The two text buttons allow you to group the listed units either by city of origin or type of unit.

**Captures:** Any units you have captured and those of yours captured and held by other nations are noted here.

**Advisors:** As on every advisor's screen, the icons for the other advisors appear to one side. Click on any one to go to that advisor's report.

## Foreign Advisor

This report is a summary of everything you know about diplomatic relations between the other civilizations with whom you have made contact, including trade arrangements and treaties. You can open this screen from the Game menu or by hitting [F4].

**Advice:** Every advisor offers advice on an ongoing basis. You might find it useful, so pay attention.

**Portraits:** This report includes small portraits of each rival ruler, including the name and title of each. The facial expression in the picture gives you a general idea of how that leader feels about you right now. Click on any leader to see that nation's relationships (those you know about) with the others, or hold the [Shift] key while clicking to

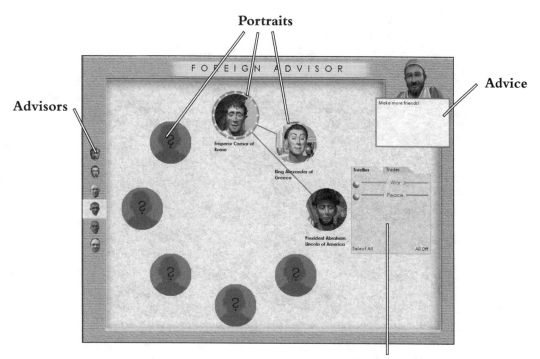

**Portraits**

**Advice**

**Advisors**

FOREIGN ADVISOR

Make more friends!

Emperor Caesar of Rome

King Alexander of Greece

President Abraham Lincoln of America

Treaties    Trades

War

Peace

Select All          All Off

**Treaty Box**

select multiple leaders. You can also double-click on any of the portraits to begin negotiations with that ruler immediately.

**Treaty box:** Using this, you control what types of agreements, treaties, and trades are shown in the circle of portraits. Select Treaties or Trades by clicking the corresponding tab, then choose the agreements you want to see. Text buttons at the bottom allow you to select all or none of the options.

**Advisors:** As on every advisor's screen, the icons for the other advisors appear to one side. Click on any one to go to that advisor's report.

## Cultural Advisor

Your nation's cultural development is vital to your success. This advisor's report gives you a one-stop summary of your empire's cultural accomplishments. You can open this screen from the Game menu or by pressing [F5].

**Culture Map**  **Total**

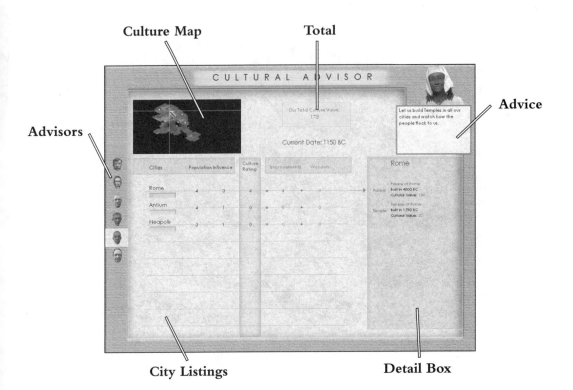

**Advisors**

**Advice**

**City Listings**  **Detail Box**

**Advice:** Every advisor offers advice on an ongoing basis. You might find it useful, so pay attention.

**Culture map:** This miniature map of the explored world includes all the cultural borders you know of. It also conveniently notes the location of the city selected in the city listings.

**Total:** For a quick overview, this box simply notes your civilization's total cultural score to date (the current date, which is listed just below the score).

**City listings:** Every one of your cities is listed here, along with a brief report on what contribution each relevant factor is making to that settlement's cultural score. The city's current cultural level is noted, and a graphic bar represents the progress toward the next level.

**Detail box:** This area displays the detailed breakdown of where the culture points for the selected city come from.

**Advisors:** As on every advisor's screen, the icons for the other advisors appear to one side. Click on any one to go to that advisor's report.

## Science Advisor

Your Science Advisor keeps a record of the advances your civilization has already achieved and the progress of your scientists toward the next advance. He presents all the possible avenues of research in the form of a handy flowchart. This chart not only shows you the research that's available to you now, it charts the entire future of science. You can open this screen from the Game menu or by hitting [F6].

**Advances**

**Advisors**

**Advice**

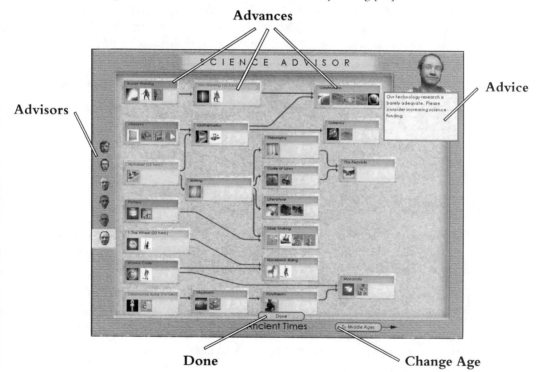

**Done**

**Change Age**

**Advice:** Every advisor offers advice on an ongoing basis. You might find it useful, so pay attention.

**Done:** This button tells your advisor that you're finished and want to return to the Map screen. If you haven't chosen an advance to research, he'll warn you about that.

**Change age:** There can be two Change Age buttons, one for the past and one for the future. Click either of these to switch to the tree for that age.

**Advances:** Each of these boxes lists one of the civilization advances that it's possible to research, and also includes icons representing any units, improvements, or Wonders of the World the advance makes possible. You can take a look at the Civilopedia entry for any advance by right-clicking on the advance. The Civilopedia entries for the units, improvements, and Wonders are also just a click away. When you decide which advance you're most interested in pursuing, just click on it. Any other advances that you need to research in order to reach your goal are selected for you and queued up. To establish a research queue manually, select the first advance (#1), then hold down the [Shift] key and select others, in the order you want them researched.

**Advisors:** As on every advisor's screen, the icons for the other advisors appear to one side. Click on any one to go to that advisor's report.

Note that it is possible to continue making advances beyond the list that defines civilization up to the present day. These continuing advances are called Future Technology, and each one you acquire adds to your Civilization Score.

# Civilopedia

The Civilopedia is an in-game encyclopedia. To open it, click the Civilopedia icon on the Map Screen. You can also see a specific entry in the Civilopedia by clicking any hyperlinked text (it's usually blue and underlined) in the game.

The entries under each topic appear alphabetically, and each includes detailed information about the item, its historical importance, and its significance in the game. The entries are also hyperlinked to each other for cross-reference purposes.

**City improvements:** This option filters the list to include only the structures you can build in a city to improve it.

**Game concepts:** This option includes all the information not covered under any of the other focused topic lists, including things like Pollution, Disbanding, and Fortresses.

**Governments:** If you want information on the various forms of government, this is the place.

**Index:** This is a complete alphabetical list of all the topics in the Civilopedia.

**Resources:** This is a complete list of all resources in the game.

**Technologies:** This option focuses on the advances. The Civilopedia entry describing each advance is also available from the Science Advisor's screen.

**Terrain:** This option provides the entries for each type of terrain square and special natural resource.

**Units:** This topic includes the entries for all units.

**Wonders:** To narrow your choices down to information about the various Wonders, use this option.

**Worker actions:** This lists all the orders you can give to Worker units.

# Wonders

This screen lists all the Wonders that have been built and any Wonders under construction that you know about. You can open this screen from the Game menu or by pressing [F7].

# Histograph

This screen displays a graphic representation of how your civilization stacks up to your opponents. It also displays your score and those of your opponents. You can open this screen from the Game menu or by hitting [F8].

**Show:** You can have the graphic comparison show each civilization's overall power rating, score, or total culture.

**Scale by:** You can have the vertical axis of the histograph scaled in years or turns.

**Score:** This displays a detailed score ranking for all civilizations, as well as more details about your own score.

# Palace

This displays your palace. At times throughout the game, your citizens will spontaneously offer to make improvements to your palace. When this happens, you select an area to improve. First, select one of the culture icons. The improvement you make will adopt the cultural appearance you choose. (These options are only available when you can make an improvement.) When you pass your mouse cursor over the potential improvement, you're given a preview of what it will look like. Click to confirm the improvement. You can open this screen from the Game menu or by pressing [F9].

# Spaceship

This screen shows the spaceship you're building to voyage to Alpha Centauri. As you complete components, you can view the progress on this display. You can open this screen from the Game menu or by hitting [F10].

**Modules, components, and structures:** When you haven't researched the required technology to build the spaceship part, each of these sections lists what advance is required. When a component is under production, the section notes what city is laboring on the project. Once the component is complete, it is listed.

**Preview:** This is a graphic display of your spaceship as it's constructed.

# Demographics

This screen displays the world's top five cities, as well as information about your citizens. You can open this screen from the Game menu or by pressing [F11].

**Top 5 Cities:** The top five cities of the world are listed, as ranked by development and size.

**Demographics:** This lists interesting facts about your population as a whole and how they rank against your opponents.

# Replay Screen

This screen allows you to replay your game from various perspectives. This is only available when you complete a game or retire.

**World Map:** This is the portion of the screen where most of the action takes place. Below the screen are four VCR-style buttons that allow you to control the replay. The information displayed is territorial control, represented by your civilization's team color. When the replay is running, you'll see the colors shift and migrate to show each civilization's piece of the world. Certain events (like Wonder construction) are called out during the replay, and the event is stored in the Event Queue.

**Histograph:** This is the portion of the screen that mirrors the functionality of the Histograph screen, with the additional feature of dynamic updating during the replay.

**Event Queue:** Events that are called out during a replay are displayed in this section of the screen.

# Preferences

The Preferences allow you to configure elements of the game to your liking. You can open this screen from the Game menu.

**Tutorial mode:** When enabled, this option displays additional helpful information for the new player.

**Always wait at end of turn:** When enabled, you will need to select End Turn each and every turn.

**Animate our manual moves:** When enabled, our units that are moved without automated orders will animate.

**Animate friendly manual moves:** When enabled, friendly units that are moved without automated orders will animate.

**Animate enemy manual moves:** When enabled, enemy units that are moved without automated orders will animate.

**Animate our automatic moves:** When enabled, our units that are moved with automated orders will animate.

**Animate friendly automatic moves:** When enabled, friendly units that are moved with automated orders will animate.

**Animate enemy automatic moves:** When enabled, enemy units that are moved with automated orders will animate.

**Animate battles:** When enabled, units engaging in combat will animate.

**Show team color disc:** When enabled, the unit's team color is displayed on a disc below the unit.

**Show food and shields on map:** When enabled, small 'tufts' are displayed on all tiles to indicate food and shield production.

**Show units over cities:** When enabled, the best defending unit in a city will be displayed over the city.

**Cancel orders when next to friend/enemy:** When enabled, our units will quit their automated order when adjacent to a friendly or enemy unit.

**Master volume slider:** Use this slider to adjust the volume of the entire game.

**Disable all sound:** Toggle this option to turn all game sound on or off.

**Music volume slider:** Use this slider to adjust the volume of the music.

**Disable music:** Toggle this option to turn all music on or off.

**SFX volume slider:** Use this slider to adjust the volume of the sound effects.

**Disable SFX:** Toggle this option to turn all sound effects on or off.

# Keyboard Shortcuts

We've mentioned these throughout the text, but it's always handy to have them listed all in one place. This is the place.

## Unit Movement

| | | |
|---|---|---|
| Move East | Right Arrow | Keypad 6 |
| Move North | Up Arrow | Keypad 8 |
| Move Northeast | Page Up | Keypad 9 |
| Move Northwest | Home | Keypad 7 |
| Move South | Down Arrow | Keypad 2 |
| Move Southeast | Page Down | Keypad 3 |
| Move Southwest | End | Keypad 1 |
| Move West | Left Arrow | Keypad 4 |

# Unit Orders

Which of these is available depends on what the active unit is, where it's standing, and its situation. For example, [B] orders a Settler to Build a City *or*, if it's standing in a city, to Join a City. Pressing [B] also tells a Worker to Build a Colony *or* Join a City; and [B] orders a Catapult to Bombard.

Please note that all of the shortcut keys are lowercase. For example, [B] means to press the "b" key. Any uppercase shortcut keys are noted as follows: [Shift]-[B].

| | |
|---|---|
| Airdrop | A |
| Airlift | T |
| Air Superiority Mission | S |
| Automate Worker | A |
| Automate, Without Altering Preexisting Improvements | Shift-A |
| Automate, This City Only | Shift-I |
| Automate, Clean Up Pollution Only | Shift-P |
| Automate, Clear Forests Only | Shift-F |
| Automate, Clear Jungle Only | Shift-J |
| Bombard | B |
| Bombing Mission | B |
| Build Army | B |
| Build City | B |
| Build Colony | B |
| Build Fortress | Ctrl-F |
| Build Mine | M |
| Build Railroad | Shift-R |
| Build Railroad To | Ctrl-Shift-R |

| | |
|---|---|
| Build Road | R |
| Build Road To | Ctrl-R |
| Build Road To, Then Colony | Ctrl-B |
| Clean Up Pollution | Shift-C |
| Clear Forest | Shift-C |
| Clear Jungle | Shift-C |
| Disband | D |
| Explore | E |
| Fortify/Garrison | F |
| GoTo | G |
| Hold (Skip Turn) | Spacebar |
| Hurry Improvement | Ctrl-H |
| Irrigate | I |
| Irrigate to Nearest City | Ctrl-I |
| Join City | B |
| Pillage | P |
| Plant Forest | N |
| Re-base Mission | Shift-R |
| Recon Mission | R |
| Trade Network | Ctrl-N |
| Unload/Load | L |
| Upgrade | U |
| Upgrade All | Shift-U |
| Wait | W or Tab |

## City Window

| | |
|---|---|
| Add to Production Queue | Shift-Click |
| Contact City Governors | G |
| Hurry Production (Rush Job) | H |
| Load Production Queue | Q |
| Save Production Queue | Shift-Q |

## Advisors

| | |
|---|---|
| Domestic Advisor | F1 |
| Trade Advisor | F2 |
| Military Advisor | F3 |
| Foreign Advisor | F4 |
| Cultural Advisor | F5 |
| Science Advisor | F6 |

## Game Stuff

| | |
|---|---|
| Center on Active Unit | C |
| Center on Capital | H |
| Change Government (Revolution) | Shift-G |
| Change Mobilization | Shift-M |
| Clean Up Map | Ctrl-Shift-M |
| Contact Rival Leaders | Shift-D |
| Demographics | F11 |
| End Turn Immediately | Shift-Enter |
| Espionage | E |
| Establish an Embassy | Ctrl-E |
| GoTo City | Ctrl-Shift-G |
| Histograph/Score | F8 |
| Locate City | Shift-L |
| Palace | F9 |
| Plant a Spy | Ctrl-Shift-E |

| | |
|---|---|
| Spaceship | F10 |
| Toggle Map Grid | Ctrl-G |
| Use Embassy or Spy | Shift-E |
| Wonders of the World | F7 |
| Zoom In/Out | Z |

## Other Stuff

| | |
|---|---|
| Change Preferences | Ctrl-P |
| Change Sound Preferences | Shift-S |
| Hide Interface | Del |
| Load Game | Ctrl-L |
| Main Menu | Ctrl-M |
| New Game | Ctrl-Shift-Q |
| Quit | Esc |
| Resign and Quit | Ctrl-Q |
| Retire | Shift-Q |
| Save Game | Ctrl-S |
| Show Game Version | Ctrl-F4 |
| Toggle Horizontal/Vertical Buttons | Backspace |

# APPENDIX A

## Units Chart

| Ancient Units | Cost (Shields) | ADM (T) BRF | Strategic Resource Required | Who Can Build (If Limited) |
|---|---|---|---|---|
| Settler | 30 | 0.0.1 | | |
| Worker | 10 | 0.0.1 | | |
| Scout | 10 | 0.0.2 | | Americans, Zulu, Iroquois, Russia, Britain |
| Warrior | 10 | 1.1.1 | | |
| *Jaguar Warrior* | *10* | *1.1.2* | | *Aztecs* |
| *Impi* | *20* | *1.2.2* | | *Zulu* |
| Spearman | 20 | 1.2.1 | | |

| Ancient Units | Cost (Shields) | ADM (T) | BRF | Strategic Resource Required | Who Can Build (If Limited) |
|---|---|---|---|---|---|
| Hoplite | 20 | 1.3.1 | | | Greeks |
| Archer | 20 | 2.1.1 | | | |
| Bowman | 20 | 2.1.2 | | | Babylonians |
| Swordsman | 30 | 3.2.1 | | Iron | |
| Legionary | 30 | 3.3.1 | | Iron | Romans |
| Immortal | 30 | 4.2.1 | | Iron | Persians |
| Horseman | 30 | 2.1.2 | | Horses | |
| Rider | 30 | 2.2.2 | | Horses | Chinese |
| Mounted Warrior | 30 | 3.1.2 | | Horses | Iroquois |
| Chariot | 20 | 1.1.2 | | Horses | |
| War Chariot | 20 | 2.1.2 | | Horses | Egyptians |
| Catapult | 20 | 0.0.1 | 4.1.1 | | |
| Galley | 30 | 1.1.3(2) | | | |

| Medieval Units | Cost (Shields) | ADM (T) | BRF | Strategic Resource Required | Who Can Build (If Limited) |
|---|---|---|---|---|---|
| Explorer | 20 | 1.1.2 | | | |
| Pikeman | 30 | 1.3.1 | | Iron | |
| Musket Man | 60 | 2.4.1 | | Saltpeter | |
| *Musketeer* | *60* | *3.4.1* | | *Saltpeter* | *French* |
| Longbowman | 40 | 4.1.1 | | | |
| Cavalry | 60 | 6.2.3 | | Horses, Saltpeter | |
| *Cossack* | *60* | *6.3.3* | | *Horses, Saltpeter* | *Russians* |
| Knight | 70 | 4.3.2 | | Iron, Horses | |
| *War Elephant* | *80* | *4.4.2* | | | *Indians* |
| *Samurai* | *80* | *5.3.2* | | *Iron* | *Japanese* |
| Cannon | 40 | 0.0.1 | 8.1.2 | Iron, Saltpeter | |
| Caravel | 40 | 1.2.3(4) | | | |
| Galleon | 60 | 1.2.4(6) | | | |
| Privateer | 60 | 2.1.4 | | Iron, Saltpeter | |
| Frigate | 60 | 2.2.4 | 2.1.2 | Iron, Saltpeter | |
| *Man-o-War* | *60* | *3.2.4* | *2.1.2* | *Iron, Saltpeter* | *British* |

| Industrial Age Units | Cost (Shields) | ADM (T) | BRF | Strategic Resource Required | Who Can Build (If Limited) |
|---|---|---|---|---|---|
| Rifleman | 80 | 3.6.1 | | | |
| Paratrooper | 100 | 8.10.1 | | Oil, Rubber | |
| Infantry | 90 | 8.12.2 | | | |
| Marines | 100 | 10.8.1 | | Oil, Rubber | |
| Tank | 100 | 16.10.2 | | Oil, Rubber | |
| *Panzer* | *100* | *16.10.3* | | *Oil, Rubber* | *Germans* |
| Artillery | 60 | 0.0.1 | 12.2.3 | | |
| Fighter | 80 | 4.4.0 | 2.0(4).2 | Oil | |
| Bomber | 100 | 0.2.0 | 8.0(6).3 | Oil | |
| Helicopter | 80 | 0.4.0(2) | 0.0(4).0 | Oil, Rubber | |
| Transport | 100 | 1.4.5(8) | | Oil | |
| Carrier | 160 | 2.8.5(4) | | Oil | |
| Iron Clad | 80 | 4.4.3 | 4.1.2 | Coal | |
| Submarine | 100 | 8.6.3 | | Oil | |
| Destroyer | 120 | 16.12.6 | 6.1.3 | Oil | |
| Battleship | 200 | 24.20.4 | 8.2.4 | Oil | |

| Modern Units | Cost (Shields) | ADM (T) | BRF | Strategic Resource Required | Who Can Build (If Limited) |
|---|---|---|---|---|---|
| Mech Infantry | 110 | 12.20.3 | | Oil, Rubber | |
| Modern Armor | 120 | 24.16.3 | | Oil, Aluminum, Rubber | |
| Radar Artillery | 80 | 0.0.1 | 16.2.4 | Aluminum | |
| Cruise Missile | 50 | 0.0.1 | 20.3.5 | Aluminum | |
| Tactical Nuke | 200 | 0.0.1 | 0.6.0 | Aluminum, Uranium | |
| ICBM | 300 | 0.0.0 | | Aluminum, Uranium | |
| Jet Fighter | 100 | 8.8.0 | 2.0(6).1 | Oil, Aluminum | |
| *F-15* | *100* | *10.8.0* | *2.0(6).1* | *Oil, Aluminum* | *Americans* |
| Stealth Fighter | 120 | 4.4.0 | 2.0(8).2 | Oil, Aluminum | |
| Stealth Bomber | 140 | 2.1.0 | 8.0(8).4 | Oil, Aluminum | |
| Nuclear Sub | 160 | 8.6.4(1) | | Uranium | |
| Aegis Cruiser | 120 | 12.12.5 | 4.2.4 | Aluminum, Uranium | |
| Army | 200 | 0.0.1(3) | | Leader or Military Academy | |
| Leader | n/a | 0.0.3 | | Victory | |

ADM(T) = Attack, Defense, Movement (Transport capacity)
BRF = Bombardment Power, Range (operational range), Rate of Fire
Note: Units in italics can only be built by a specific civilization (for example, *F-15* by *Americans*).

# Terrain Charts

| | Food | Shields | Commerce | Irrigate (+ Food) | Mine (+ Shields) | Road (+ Commerce) |
|---|---|---|---|---|---|---|
| **Flood Plains** | 3 | – | – | +1 | – | +1 |
| **Grasslands** | 2 | – | – | +1 | +1 | +1 |
| **Plains** | 1 | 1 | – | +1 | +1 | +1 |
| **Desert** | – | 1 | – | +1 | +1 | +1 |
| **Tundra** | 1 | – | – | – | +1 | +1 |
| **Forest** | 1 | 2 | – | – | – | +1 |
| **Jungle** | 1 | – | – | – | – | +1 |
| **Hills** | 1 | 1 | – | – | +2 | +1 |
| **Mountains** | – | 1 | – | – | +2 | +1 |
| **Coast** | 1 | – | 2 | – | – | – |
| **Sea** | 1 | – | 1 | – | – | – |
| **Ocean** | 1 | – | – | – | – | – |

| Bonus Resources | Strategic Resources | Luxury Resources | Movement Cost | Defense Value |
|---|---|---|---|---|
| Wheat | – | – | 1 | 10 |
| Cattle, Wheat | Horses | Wine | 1 | 10 |
| Cattle, Wheat | Horses, Iron, Oil, Aluminum | Wine, Ivory | 1 | 10 |
| – | Saltpeter, Oil | Incense | 1 | 10 |
| Cattle, Game | Saltpeter, Oil | Fur | 1 | 10 |
| Game | Uranium, Rubber | Dye, Spice, Ivory, Silk | 2 | 25 |
| Game | Rubber | Dye, Spice, Silk, Gems | 3 | 25 |
| Gold | Horses, Iron, Saltpeter, Coal, Aluminum | Wine, Incense | 2 | 50 |
| Gold | Iron, Saltpeter, Coal, Aluminum, Uranium | Gems | 3 | 100 |
| Fish | – | – | 1 | 10 |
| Whale, Fish | – | – | 1 | 10 |
| Whale, Fish | – | – | 1 | 10 |

## Consumable Goods

|         | Food | Shields | Commerce |
|---------|------|---------|----------|
| Cattle  | +2   | +1      | –        |
| Fish    | +2   | –       | +1       |
| Game    | +1   | –       | –        |
| Whales  | +1   | +1      | +2       |
| Wheat   | +2   | –       | –        |
| Gold    | —    | —       | +4       |

## Strategic Resources

|           | Food | Shields | Commerce |
|-----------|------|---------|----------|
| Aluminum  | –    | +2      | –        |
| Coal      | –    | +2      | +1       |
| Horses    | –    | –       | +1       |
| Iron      | –    | +1      | –        |
| Oil       | –    | +1      | +2       |
| Rubber    | –    | –       | +2       |
| Saltpeter | –    | –       | +1       |
| Uranium   | –    | +2      | +3       |

# Luxury Resources

| | Food | Shields | Commerce |
|---|---|---|---|
| Dyes | – | – | +1 |
| Furs | – | +1 | +1 |
| Gems | – | – | +4 |
| Incense | – | – | +1 |
| Ivory | – | – | +2 |
| Silk | – | – | +3 |
| Spice | – | – | +2 |
| Wines | +1 | – | +1 |

# TECHNICAL SUPPORT (U.S. AND CANADA)

## Help Via the Internet

Up-to-the-minute technical information about Infogrames Interactive products is generally available 24 hours a day, 7 days a week via the Internet at:

**http://www.ina-support.com**

Through this site you'll have access to our **FAQ** (Frequently Asked Questions) documents, our **FTP** (File Transfer Protocol) area where you can download patches if needed, our **Hints/Cheat Codes** if they're available, and an **E-Mail** area where you can get help and ask questions if you do not find your answers within the **FAQ**.

## Help Via Telephone/Fax or Mail in the United States and Canada

For phone assistance, call Infogrames Interactive **Tech Support** at **(425) 951-7108**. Our **Interactive Voice Response** and **Faxback** system is generally available 24/7, providing automated support and allowing FAQ documents to be faxed to you immediately. Live support is available Monday through Friday, 8:00 AM until 6:00 PM (Pacific Time). **Note:** We may be closed on major holidays.

Before making your call, we ask that you be at your computer, have the following information available, and be ready to take notes:

- System make and model

- Processor type

- Operating system, including version number if possible (such as Windows® 95 or Windows® Me)

- RAM (memory)

- Any screen or error messages you've encountered (and where)

You may also fax in your Technical Support questions or problems to **(425) 806–0480**, or write to the address below.

## Product Return Procedures in the United States and Canada

In the event our technicians at **(425) 951–7108** determine that you need to forward materials directly to us, please include a brief letter explaining what is enclosed and why. Make sure you include the Return Merchandise Authorization Number (RMA#) supplied to you by the technician, and your telephone number in case we need to call you. Any materials not containing this RMA# will be returned to you unprocessed. Send your materials to the following address:

Infogrames Interactive, Inc.

Attn: TS/CS Dept.

13110 NE 177th Place

Suite # B101, Box 180

Woodinville, WA 98072-9965

RMA #

# INFOGRAMES WEB SITES

The *Civilization III* CD-ROM game has an exciting, full and active web site dedicated to ensure you get the most out of your new game. You can visit us at:

## http://www.civ3.com

Kids, check with your parent or guardian before visiting any web site.

Visit and you will discover that Infogrames web sites contain such things as:

- Technical Support

- Hints and Tips

- Demos

- Interviews

- Competitions

- Community

- And much more

We are constantly updating our web sites so stop by and visit us frequently. With events and new additions planned, you won't want to miss out.

# Forthcoming and Existing Infogrames Products

For more information on forthcoming and other existing Infogrames products, please visit our main web site at:

**http://www.us.infogrames.com**

# LICENSE
# AGREEMENT

## *** IMPORTANT ***

This is a legal agreement between the end user ("You") and Infogrames Interactive, Inc., its parent, affiliates and subsidiaries (collectively "Infogrames Interactive"). This Agreement is part of a package (the "Package") that also includes, as applicable, executable files that you may download, a game cartridge or disc, or a CD-ROM (collectively referred to herein as the "Software") and certain written materials (the "Documentation"). Any patch, update, upgrade, modification or other enhancement provided by Infogrames Interactive with respect to the Software or the Documentation, or bonus game provided by Infogrames Interactive at no extra charge as part of the Package, shall be included within the meanings of those terms, for the purposes of this Agreement, except to the extent expressly provided below.

BY DOWNLOADING OR INSTALLING THE SOFTWARE, YOU ACKNOWLEDGE THAT YOU HAVE READ ALL OF THE TERMS AND CONDITIONS OF THIS AGREEMENT, UNDERSTAND THEM, AND AGREE TO BE BOUND BY THEM. YOU UNDERSTAND THAT, IF YOU PURCHASED THE PACKAGE FROM AN AUTHORIZED RESELLER OF INFOGRAMES INTERACTIVE, THAT RESELLER IS NOT INFOGRAMES INTERACTIVE'S AGENT AND IS NOT AUTHORIZED TO MAKE ANY REPRESENTATIONS, CONDITIONS OR WARRANTIES, STATUTORY OR OTHERWISE, ON INFOGRAMES INTERACTIVE'S BEHALF NOR TO VARY ANY OF THE TERMS OR CONDITIONS OF THIS AGREEMENT.

If You do not agree to the terms of this Agreement, do not download or install the Software and promptly return the entire Package to the place You obtained it for a full refund. If you should have any difficulty in obtaining such refund, please contact Infogrames Interactive Technical Support at 425-951-7108. Failure to return the entire Package within 30 days of the purchase date shall be presumed to constitute acceptance of the terms and conditions of this Agreement.

# CONSUMER SAFETY WARNINGS AND PRECAUTIONS STATEMENT:

## Epilepsy Warning

⚠️ **WARNING**

# READ THIS NOTICE BEFORE YOU OR YOUR CHILD USE THIS SOFTWARE

A very small portion of the population have a condition which may cause them to experience epileptic seizures or have momentary loss of consciousness when viewing certain kinds of flashing lights or patterns. These persons may experience seizures while watching some kinds of television pictures or playing certain video games. Certain conditions may induce previously undetected epileptic symptoms even in persons who have no history of prior seizures or epilepsy.

If you or anyone in your family has an epileptic condition or has experienced symptoms like an epileptic condition (e.g. a seizure or loss of awareness), immediately consult your physician before using this Software.

We recommend that parents observe their children while they play games. If you or your child experience any of the following symptoms: dizziness, altered vision, eye or muscle twitching, involuntary movements, loss of awareness, disorientation, or convulsions, **DISCONTINUE USE IMMEDIATELY** and consult your physician.

# FOLLOW THESE PRECAUTIONS WHENEVER USING THIS SOFTWARE:

- Do not sit or stand too close to the monitor. Play as far back from the monitor as possible.

- Do not play if you are tired or need sleep.

- Always play in a well-lit room.

- Be sure to take a 10- to 15-minute break every hour while playing.

## Repetitive Strain Statement

⚠ **CAUTION**

Some people may experience fatigue or discomfort after playing for a long time. Regardless of how you feel, you should ALWAYS take a 10- to 15-minute break every hour while playing. If your hands or arms become tired or uncomfortable while playing, stop and rest. If you continue to experience soreness or discomfort during or after play, listen to the signals your body is giving you. Stop playing and consult a doctor. Failure to do so could result in long term injury.

If your hands, wrist or arms have been injured or strained in other activities, use of this Software could aggravate the condition. Before playing, consult a doctor.

## Motion Sickness Statement

⚠ **CAUTION**

This Software generates realistic images and 3-D simulations. While playing or watching certain video images, some people may experience dizziness, motion sickness or nausea. If you or your child experience any of these symptoms, discontinue use and play again later.

**LIMITED LICENSE:** You are entitled to download or install, and operate this Software solely for your own personal use, but may not sell or transfer reproductions of the Software or Documentation to other parties in any way. You may download or install, and operate one copy of the Software on a single terminal connected to a single computer. You may not network the Software or otherwise use it on more than one computer or computer terminal at the same time.

**INTERNET-BASED PLAY; CHAT:** This Software may include Internet-play features. If You choose to use such features, You will need to access the Internet. The Software or Documentation may also suggest links to certain Software-related web sites, including web sites operated by Infogrames Interactive or third parties. Your access to web sites operated by Infogrames Interactive is subject to the terms of use and privacy policies of such web sites. Children should check with a parent or guardian before accessing the Internet, including without limitation any chat function, on-line "arcade," or em@il Game. Internet game play may occur through one or more independent gaming or other web sites (each a "Web Site"), including without limitation the MSN Gaming Zone run by the Microsoft Corporation. Infogrames Interactive does not review or control, and disclaims any responsibility or liability for, the functioning and performance of any Web Site, the terms of use of any Web Site, the privacy policies of any Web Site, and any content on or available via a Web Site, including, without limitation, links to other web sites and comments or other contact between users of a Web Site. Infogrames Interactive does not endorse the Web Sites merely because a link to the Web Site is suggested or established. Infogrames Interactive does not monitor, control, endorse, or accept responsibility for the content of text or voice chat messages, if applicable, transmitted through the use of the Software. Use of the chat function, or other content or services of any Web Site is at Your own risk. You are strongly encouraged not to give out identity or other personal information through chat transmissions.

**OWNERSHIP; COPYRIGHT:** Title to the Software and the Documentation, and patents, copyrights and all other property rights applicable thereto, shall at all times remain solely and exclusively with Infogrames Interactive and its licensors, and You shall not take any action inconsistent with such title. The Software and the Documentation are protected by United States, Canadian and other applicable laws and by international treaty provisions. Any rights not expressly granted herein are reserved to Infogrames Interactive and its licensors.

**OTHER RESTRICTIONS:** You may not cause or permit the disclosure, copying, renting, licensing, sublicensing, leasing, dissemination or other distribution of the Software or the Documentation by any means or in any form, without the prior written consent of Infogrames Interactive. You may not modify, enhance, supplement, create derivative work from, adapt, translate, reverse engineer, decompile, disassemble or otherwise reduce the Software to human readable form.

**LIMITED WARRANTY:**

Infogrames Interactive warrants for a period of ninety (90) days following original retail purchase of this copy of the Software that the Software is free from substantial errors or defects that will materially interfere with the operation of the Software as described in the Documentation. This limited warranty: (i) applies to the initial purchaser only and may be acted upon only by the initial purchaser; and (ii) does not apply to any patch, update, upgrade, modification, or other enhancement provided by Infogrames Interactive with respect to the Software or the Documentation or to any bonus game provided by Infogrames Interactive at no extra charge as part of the Package, which are provided on an AS IS BASIS ONLY. EXCEPT AS STATED ABOVE, INFOGRAMES INTERACTIVE AND ITS LICENSORS MAKE NO OTHER WARRANTY OR CONDITION, EXPRESS OR IMPLIED, STATUTORY OR OTHERWISE, REGARDING THIS SOFTWARE. THE IMPLIED WARRANTY THAT THE SOFTWARE IS FIT FOR A PARTICULAR PURPOSE AND THE IMPLIED WARRANTY OF MERCHANTABILITY SHALL BOTH BE LIMITED TO THE NINETY (90) DAY DURATION OF THIS LIMITED EXPRESS WARRANTY. THESE AND ANY OTHER IMPLIED WARRANTIES OR CONDITIONS, STATUTORY OR OTHERWISE, ARE OTHERWISE EXPRESSLY AND SPECIFICALLY DISCLAIMED. Some jurisdictions do not allow limitations on how long an implied warranty or condition lasts, so the above limitation may not apply to You. This limited warranty gives You specific legal rights, and you may also have other rights which vary from jurisdiction to jurisdiction.

If you believe you have found any such error or defect in the Software during the warranty period, call Infogrames Interactive Technical Support at 425-951-7108 between the hours of 8:00 a.m. and 6:00 p.m. Monday through Friday (Pacific Time), holidays excluded, and provide your Product number. If a return is determined as necessary, a Return Merchandise Authorization Number (RMA#) will be issued to you. Send your original CD-ROM disc, game cartridge or disc, or, if applicable, the executable files that you downloaded, along with the RMA#, a dated proof of purchase, your full name, address and phone number, to Infogrames Interactive, Inc., Attn: TS/CS Dept., 13110 NE 177th Place, Suite # B101, Box 180, Woodinville, WA 98072-9965.

If you have a problem resulting from a manufacturing defect in the Software, Infogrames Interactive's and its licensors' entire liability and Your exclusive remedy for breach of this limited warranty shall be the replacement of the Software, within a reasonable period of time and without charge, with a corrected version of the Software. Some jurisdictions do not allow the exclusion or limitation of relief, incidental or consequential damages, so the above limitation or exclusion may not apply to You.

## LIMITATION OF LIABILITY:

INFOGRAMES INTERACTIVE AND ITS LICENSORS SHALL NOT BE LIABLE FOR SPECIAL, INCIDENTAL, CONSEQUENTIAL, EXEMPLARY OR OTHER INDIRECT DAMAGES, EVEN IF INFOGRAMES INTERACTIVE OR ITS LICENSORS ARE ADVISED OF OR AWARE OF THE POSSIBILITY OF SUCH DAMAGES. IN NO EVENT SHALL INFOGRAMES INTERACTIVE'S AND ITS LICENSORS' AGGREGATE LIABILITY EXCEED THE PURCHASE PRICE OF THIS PACKAGE. Some jurisdictions do not allow the exclusion or limitation of special, incidental, consequential, indirect or exemplary damages, or the limitation of liability to specified amounts, so the above limitation or exclusion may not apply to You.

**GENERAL:** This Agreement constitutes the entire understanding between Infogrames Interactive and You with respect to subject matter hereof. Any change to this Agreement must be in writing, signed by Infogrames Interactive and You. Terms and conditions as set forth in any purchase order which differ from, conflict with, or are not included in this Agreement, shall not become part of this Agreement unless specifically accepted by Infogrames Interactive in writing. You shall be responsible for and shall pay, and shall reimburse Infogrames Interactive on request if Infogrames Interactive is required to pay, any sales, use, value added (VAT), consumption or other tax (excluding any tax that is based on Infogrames Interactive's net income), assessment, duty, tariff, or other fee or charge of any kind or nature that is levied or imposed by any governmental authority on the Package.

**EXPORT AND IMPORT COMPLIANCE:** In the event You export the Software or the Documentation from the country in which You first received it, You assume the responsibility for compliance with all applicable export and re-export regulations, as the case may be.

**GOVERNING LAW; ARBITRATION:** This Agreement shall be governed by, and any arbitration hereunder shall apply, the laws of the State of New York, U.S.A., excluding (a) its conflicts of laws principles; (b) the United Nations Convention on Contracts for the International Sale of Goods; (c) the 1974 Convention on the Limitation Period in the International Sale of Goods (the "1974 Convention"); and (d) the Protocol amending the 1974 Convention, done at Vienna April 11, 1980.

Any dispute, controversy or claim arising out of or relating to this Agreement or to a breach hereof, including its interpretation, performance or termination, shall be finally resolved by arbitration. The arbitration shall be conducted by three (3) arbitrators, one to be appointed by Infogrames Interactive, one to be appointed by You and a third being nominated by the two arbitrators so selected or, if they cannot agree on a third arbitrator, by the President of the American Arbitration Association ("AAA"). The arbitration shall be conducted in English and in accordance with the commercial arbitration rules of the AAA. The arbitration, including the rendering of the award, shall take place in New York, New York, and shall be the exclusive forum for resolving such dispute, controversy or claim. The decision of the arbitrators shall be binding upon the parties hereto, and the expense of the arbitration (including without limitation the award of attorneys' fees to the prevailing party) shall be paid as the arbitrators determine. The decision of the arbitrators shall be executory, and judgment thereon may be entered by any court of competent jurisdiction.

Notwithstanding anything contained in the foregoing Paragraph to the contrary, Infogrames Interactive shall have the right to institute judicial proceedings against You or anyone acting by, through or under You, in order to enforce Infogrames Interactive's rights hereunder through reformation of contract, specific performance, injunction or similar equitable relief. For the purposes of this Paragraph, both parties submit to the jurisdiction of, and waive any objection to the venue of, the state and federal courts of the State of New York.

# CREDITS

## Original CIVILIZATION Designed By

Sid Meier

## CIVILIZATION III Designed By

Jeff Briggs,
Soren Johnson, and
Members of FIRAXIS GAMES

*Programming*
David Evans
Soren Johnson
Mike Breitkreutz
Jacob Solomon
Patrick Dawson
Javier Sobrado
Chris Pine

*Art*
Nicholas Rusko-Berger, Lead
Jerome Atherholt
Michael Bazzell
Alex Kim
Ryan Murray
Kevin Margo
Dorian Newcomb
Michael Bates
Brent Alleyne
Marc Hudgins
Gregory Foerstch
Justin Thomas
Jon Marro

*Sound*
Mark Cromer

*Music*
Roger Briggs
Mark Cromer

*Production*
Mike Gibson
Jeff Morris
Mike Fetterman, Associate

*Writers*
John Possidente, Manual
Paul Murphy, Diplomacy dialogues
Rex Martin, Civilopedia
Jason Gleason, Civilopedia

*Firaxis Marketing*
Lindsay Riehl
Kelley Gilmore
Dan Magaha

*Additional Art*
Carlson Bull
David Austin

# Infogrames Interactive, Inc.

**Senior Producer**
Thomas J. Zahorik

**Executive Producer**
Bill Levay

**Senior Marketing Product Manager**
Peter Matiss

**V.P. of Product Development**
Scott Walker

**General Manager**
John Hurlbut

**Director of Quality Assurance**
Michael Craighead

**Q.A. Certification Manager**
Kurt Boutin

**Q.A. Testing Managers**
Mark Gutknecht
Randy Lee
Bill Carroll

**Q.A. Certification Lead**
Michael Davidson

**Lead Testers**
Grant Frazier
Rex Martin

**Testers**
Barry Caudill
Ellie Crawley
Jason Gleason
Brad Hoppenstein
Kevin Jamieson
Tim McCracken
Ray Pfeifer
Steve Purdie

Jeff Smith
Shawn Walbeck

**Director of Marketing**
Ann Marie Bland

**Manager of Creative Services**
Steve Martin

**Manager of Editorial &
Documentation Services**
Elizabeth Mackney

**Graphic Designer**
Paul Anselmi

**Editor**
Marisa Ong

**Manual Designer**
William Salit Design

## Special Thanks

Alex Delucia
Rex Martin
Jason Gleason
Ellie Crawley
Barry Caudill
Andy Mazurek
…and the families of everyone
involved

222

# INDEX

# B

# C

# I

# K

# L

# M

# Stuck? Stumped?

Help is at your fingertips!
Hints, tips and how to get a
Strategy Guide are just a
phone call away.

## CALL 1-900-454-HINT

$.99 per minute

08251